For my mom, Cameron, Casey, Melanie, and Summer—the women who taught me strength, trust, and confidence. And for Ann Marie who keeps me reaching higher.

"Courtney has given us a practical and personal resource to know and experience God's beauty and presence in our own lives. Courtney writes with humility and wisdom; I greatly appreciate her research, examples, and helpful instruction to honor God through the care of our body, mind, and soul."

—**Travis Osborne**,
Lead Pastor, Valley Christian Family

"God has created the human body with a perfect design to heal. Through biblical text and heartfelt wisdom, Courtney lays out the body-mind-soul holistic model and helps you move through what might be standing between you and radiant health at every level."

— **Jennifer Galardi**,
Health and Wellness Expert | Policy Writer

"This book is nothing short of deeply impactful. With every page, it feels holy in its commitment to fostering a connection between the body and soul. Courtney's insight strikes at the core of what it means to live a balanced, purposeful life, drawing from a deep well of life-giving advice and leadership. It's a transformative read that inspires not only personal growth but also a sense of shared humanity. A must-read for anyone seeking meaningful, soulful connection in their everyday life."

— **Ericka Jones**,
Chief Connector and Community Builder

"A refreshing reset to know and feel God's love and purpose through intentional physical, mental, and spiritual actions. A personal insight to realigning your faith, family, and friendships while knowing and experiencing God's beauty and presence in your life."

—**Alison Hall,**
First Lady of Simpson University and Director of Student Teaching

"In *Move into Meaning*, Courtney beautifully weaves her personal journey with the actionable steps that have deepened her connection with God. This transformational book will inspire you to draw closer to God and discover a more meaningful relationship with yourself."

—**Aaron Hayes,**
Leadership Consultant and Pastor

"Courtney does a brilliant job expounding upon biblical wisdom and its direct correlation to living a whole, restful, mindful life. The practical weekly applications are tailored to lead you into a life of surrender, serenity, and self-awareness."

— **Brittany Baer,**
Business Owner and Writer | Founder of Gild Beauty Bar

MOVE INTO MEANING

ESSENTIAL SPIRITUAL EXERCISES FOR A FULFILLED LIFE

Courtney McElvain

LUCIDBOOKS

Move Into Meaning
Essential Spiritual Exercises for a Fulfilled Life
A 12-week Program
Copyright © 2025 by Courtney McElvain

Published by Lucid Books in Houston, TX
www.LucidBooks.com

All rights reserved. No part of this publication may be reproduced, stored in a retrieval system, or transmitted in any form by any means, electronic, mechanical, photocopy, recording, or otherwise, without the prior permission of the publisher, except as provided for by USA copyright law.

Unless otherwise indicated, scripture quotations are taken from the (NLT) Holy Bible, New Living Translation, copyright ©1996, 2004, 2015 by Tyndale House Foundation. Used by permission of Tyndale House Publishers, Carol Stream, Illinois 60188. All rights reserved.

eISBN: 978-1-63296-792-3
ISBN: 978-1-63296-791-6

Special Sales: Most Lucid Books titles are available in special quantity discounts. Custom imprinting or excerpting can also be done to fit special needs. Contact Lucid Books at Info@LucidBooks.com

To protect the privacy of individuals, some names and identifying details in this book have been changed. Any resemblance to actual persons, living or deceased, is purely coincidental unless otherwise explicitly stated.

This book includes suggested stretches and exercises intended to promote physical wellness. Readers are strongly encouraged to consult with a physician or healthcare provider before beginning any new exercise program, especially if you have any existing health conditions or injuries. The authors and publishers are not liable for any injuries or health issues that may result from following the exercises presented.

TABLE OF CONTENTS

Introduction	1
SECTION 1: "Love the Lord Your God with All Your Heart"	11
Chapter 1: The Art and Science of Us	13
God's Ultimate Masterpiece	15
Our Body Is Our Temple	16
God Breathes – We Breathe	19
Restful Breath Exercise	20
Quieting Ourselves	21
Actions and Reactions	23
Recap	24
Activities Week 1	25
Chapter 2: Temple Body Power	27
Honoring Our Temple Body with a Body Mindset	29
Honoring Our Temple Body with Food	33
Honoring Our Temple Body with Exercise	35
Honoring Our Temple Bodies with Rest	42
The Action-Rest Tension	44
Activities Week 2	45
Chapter 3: The Power of Intention	47
Let's Pretend . . .	48
Moses in the Rock	52
Call on His Name	56
The Futures We Create	58
Recap	59
Activities Week 3	60

SECTION 2: "Love the Lord Your God with All Your Mind" — 63
Chapter 4: Inner Thoughts and Consciousness — 65
    Active Consciousness — 66
    Renewing Our Mind — 68
    Sympathetic and Parasympathetic Nervous Systems — 69
    The Tummy (Solar Plexus) — 71
    The Vagus Nerve — 72
    The Diaphragm — 72
    Taking Action to Bring It Together — 73
    God's Prescription When You Feel Overwhelmed — 74
    Recap of God's 8-Step Prescription — 77
    Pay Attention to Your Thoughts — 78
    Activities Week 4 — 80
Chapter 5: Prayer and God's Timing — 83
    Enter Babylon — 87
    For Such a Time as This — 90
    God's Time – Our Time — 93
    A Blueprint for Inner Work — 96
    The Treasure in Our Hearts — 99
    Activities Week 5 — 101
Chapter 6: Reflecting the Creator Through Mind-Body Techniques — 103
    Meditation — 104
    Yoga — 107
    Breath Work — 111
    Reflecting Our Creator — 112
    Activities Week 6 — 115

SECTION 3: "Love the Lord your God with all your Soul" — 117
Chapter 7: From Darkness to Light — 119
    Plato's Cave and a Life in Christ — 121
    Soul Versus Spirit — 121
    Saul's Spiritual Rebirth — 123

Fasting and Reflection	124
The Ceremony of Baptism	127
Living As Light	129
Activities Week 7	130
Chapter 8: Patterns and Purpose	**133**
God's Equipping Power	134
Opportunity and Courage Meet	137
Two Kinds of Strength	140
Courage and Trust	140
The Pattern of God's Beauty	141
Redemption: God's Grand Design	142
Two Ways to Live Out God's Design Today	143
Activities Week 8	144
Chapter 9: The Yet Theory	**147**
The Maturing of Faith	148
Finding Meaning in Life	149
Thankfulness: Our Sacrifice	152
The Yet Theory	153
Remember	154
Clouds: God's Presence	157
Activities Week 9	160
SECTION 4: "Love Your Neighbor as Yourself"	**161**
Chapter 10: The Wonder of Love and Our Relational Design	**163**
When Loving Others Feels Difficult	164
In Search of Our Identity	165
The Design of Relationship: Unveiling the Trinity	166
How the Trinity Shapes Our Relationships	168
Connecting to God	171
Church Hurt: Finding Trust and Faith Again	173
Why the Church Is Essential	174
The Body of Christ	175
The Healing Power of Group Confession	177

Helping and Encouraging One Another	177
Church: Where We Live Out the Natural Order of Love	178
Activities Week 10	179
Chapter 11: Subtraction and the Art of Letting Go	**183**
The Cost of A Hurried Life	185
Freedom Through Humility	186
The Subtlety of Conviction	188
The Enemies Working against Us	190
King David's Confession	191
Letting Go of Burdens and Distractions	193
Examen Prayer: A Powerful Practice for Daily Renewal	194
The Art of Forgiveness	195
Space for the Soul to Breathe	197
Activities Week 11	198
Chapter 12: Generosity and Blessings	**201**
Tying It All Together	202
Two Stories of Radical Generosity	203
Acts of Service	204
Returning Home	206
A Blessing to You	206
Final Words	**208**
Acknowledgments	**209**
Endnotes	**211**

INTRODUCTION

On my nightstand sits a volume that includes Lewis Carroll's novel, *Alice's Adventures in Wonderland,* and the sequel, *Through the Looking Glass.* It's my favorite book of all time. The cover itself is a work of art; it's purple, puffy, and matte textured. And Alice appears to be falling headfirst in slow motion beside the white rabbit; both characters are embossed and smooth in silvery shades of purple. But the stories the volume holds are its best feature; they are a metaphor for how I see the world at this stage in my life.[1]

I've grown beyond Disney's 1951 version of *Alice in Wonderland,* which I recall from my childhood and perceive the story more philosophically today. When I was a kid, the quirky characters and image of Alice with her blonde hair and black headband stuck out the most. Today, I see the storyline as a reminder that things aren't always what they seem. This is both a warning and an invitation. We're invited and hold a responsibility to think differently about the way things are presented to us. And we're designed with the creativity and minds to do so. These stories are also a reminder that the adventures of this world are more colorful and fun when you surround yourself with people who are entirely bonkers.

I was born with all the sharp edges of a Type A personality. Before 2020, I thrived on outcomes, willing to do whatever it took to ensure success, even if it meant being demanding, curt, or frustrated with those around me. I didn't think that was a problem; my achievements were met with applause, and any toll my style took on relationships felt subtle enough to ignore.

But 2020 was a tipping point. My husband served as our town's mayor during this tumultuous time, while I faced challenges as a wealth manager navigating client fears during a stock market freefall. At home, we pulled our two children from school because of struggles with distance learning and took on homeschooling with friends. The weight of it all caught up with me in December when a piercing headache turned out to be shingles in my left eye. My doctor didn't mince words: "Take it easy for three months, or risk losing your vision," he advised. It was a stark wake-up call for me to reevaluate the relentless pace and priorities I had clung to for so long.

But I was angry. Three months? I was being forced to stop, and I couldn't make sense of it. I felt betrayed by my own body. I had always pushed through every challenge, never letting anything or anyone stop me. As an Army veteran, I was no stranger to discipline and perseverance. My life was full, supported by strong routines and structure. I helped others reach their goals, taught fitness and yoga for decades, ate well, exercised daily; I stayed grounded with journaling, Bible reading, and prayer. Surely, I thought, I could just power through this like I always had, and it would resolve itself. Who did I think I

INTRODUCTION

was? Trapped in a Type A mindset, I left no room for rest. With love and gentleness, my husband of over two decades sat me down and encouraged me to stop. He suggested no going to the office, no board and committee meetings, no driving the kids around. Just two weeks to tend to myself. Reluctantly, I agreed. To my surprise, I began to feel a glimmer of hope, like a tiny seed of excitement deep inside me. I felt a bit like curious Alice stepping through the looking glass; watching the world I knew dissolve into a silvery mist; and landing softly, warmly, on the other side. For the first time, I wondered if letting go could lead to something new.

Everyone has their 2020 story. That was mine.

It didn't take me long into the two-week window of rest to truly know that the shingles weren't something that happened to me, but for me. Shingles was a gift. And I felt ashamed of my initial attitude about it all. Of course, something like this could happen, and much worse, to any of us. It's life.

That two-week window opened my eyes to shifting priorities. By putting on the brakes and removing myself physically, mentally, and emotionally from my everyday life, I began my journey to operate at a whole new frequency. This was not a vacation. It was not about "getting away from it all" like traveling in a new city exploring attractions and a new culture. It also wasn't a staycation for catching up on things in life outside of work. My intent for stopping was removal and rest—about being instead of doing. It was about being agenda-less and de-stimulating. I ended up spending time in activities that opened my eyes to fresh thoughts and ideas. I spent time with God one-on-one, staying quiet enough to hear His still, small voice. I caught up with my soul. Everything within my physical body that needed release released, and my body began to heal.

I began learning that latent potential within me could be unleashed if I created margin in my life. But that was not something I could force or plan. By my doing nothing, God was doing something. By turning myself down, I turned God up. And by doing so, I was able to experience His goodness in a new way.

This book is about experiencing God in a whole new way, and it's centered around Jesus's words in Matthew 22:37–39: *"'You must love the LORD your God with all your heart, all your soul, and all your mind.' This is the first and greatest commandment. A second is equally important: 'Love your neighbor as yourself.'"*

God wants us to love Him with our everything—to prefer Him over everything. But how do we do that in today's world? As moms, dads, husbands, wives, and professionals, how do we make time for God in a way that is meaningful? For the last ten years, that's the question I've been sorting through, reading about, thinking on, journaling on, and talking through with other followers of Jesus. My shingles experience was the kick I needed to finally put pen to paper and put into order my chaotic thoughts on this topic.

How do we love God with our whole heart, mind, and soul in the full and distracted lives we live today? How do we love others as God does? The insights and spiritual exercises in this book are my answer to these questions. And the incredible thing is this: God's guidance and instruction always come at just the right moment, from the womb to the tomb. His timing is flawless. You're holding this book in your hands right now because this is the perfect moment for you to receive this message.

INTRODUCTION

The birth of this book was inspired by ideas I discovered in books written by Dallas Willard and Richard Foster. In *Living in Christ's Presence*, John Ortberg interviews Dallas Willard who taught me how to define the parts of a person by looking closely at the passage from Matthew 22:37–39. Willard and Ortberg helped me understand how our lives can change by focusing on each part of our person separately and training it.[2] So, I divided *Move Into Meaning* into four sections based on the parts of our person: heart, mind, soul, and loving others. The common thread you will find throughout *Move Into Meaning* is its focus on the movement of God in our lives, in others, and in the world around us. The goal is to look for where God is at work making changes in our lives and to join Him in that work. It's about developing the energy and intentionality to care about how He is moving in the lives of others and aligning ourselves with His purpose. Ultimately, it's about finding deeper meaning in our own lives by participating in His movement, sharing His love, and being a part of something far greater than ourselves.

The second book that inspired me to write *Move Into Meaning* was Richard Foster's *Celebration of Discipline: The Path to Spiritual Growth*. Foster includes twelve spiritual disciplines, or spiritual exercises as I like to call them, that will aid in deepening our relationship with God. He breaks them down into three categories: inward disciplines, outward disciplines, and corporate disciplines.

- Inward disciplines include: (1) meditation, (2) prayer, (3) fasting, and (4) study.

- Outward disciplines are: (1) simplicity, (2) solitude, (3) submission, and (4) service.
- Corporate disciplines: (1) confession, (2) worship, (3) guidance, and (4) celebration.[3]

Foster's book provided a loose framework for the spiritual exercises woven throughout *Move Into Meaning*. We'll begin with the deeply personal, exploring what it means to treat our bodies as temples of the Holy Spirit, honoring God in the way we live, think, and care for ourselves. But it doesn't stop there. As temples, we remain uniquely created individuals with our own purpose and gifts. Yet, we're also called to something greater—to become part of the collective body of Christ. From the personal, we move to the communal, discovering how our individual lives connect to the larger, living body of believers. But this isn't about losing individuality; it's about understanding how God's design allows us to retain our uniqueness while becoming part of something much bigger. Together we'll explore what it means to live as individuals fully aligned with God while contributing to the shared mission, unity, and love of Christ's body.

Section 1, loving God with all our heart, explores both the physical heart of our cardiovascular system and the symbolic heart, focusing on treating our bodies as temples. We'll discover how physical and spiritual health are deeply connected. Caring for ourselves through good nutrition, exercise, restful sleep, and a positive mindset isn't just about feeling good; it's about honoring God and aligning our whole selves with His purpose. Through Scripture and personal stories, we'll see how nurturing our bodies helps us live more fully in the life God has designed for us.

INTRODUCTION

Section 2, loving God with all our mind, dives into the powerful connection between our thoughts, emotions, actions, and relationship with Him. Through examples like Dorian Gray's struggles and Elijah's renewal, we'll uncover how to break negative patterns and align our minds with God's truth. We'll also look at Esther's story, discovering how trusting God's timing can shape the future. Using insights from Scripture, neuroscience, and practices such as prayer, meditation, yoga, and breath work, this section encourages you to clear mental clutter and make space for God to fill you with His power and courage.

In section 3, loving God with all our soul, we'll dive into the soul's vital role in spiritual growth, resilience, and transformation. Using stories like Plato's *Allegory of the Cave* and Saul's powerful conversion, we'll explore the journey from darkness to light, reflecting life in Christ. We'll also take a closer look at how courage takes on different forms of strength through the lives of Deborah and Jael. With practices such as fasting, prayer, and small acts of faith, you'll be encouraged to care for your soul, embrace God's redemptive design, and reflect His love to others. We'll also explore "The Yet Theory," discovering how even in struggles and tragedy, there's an opportunity for growth and a deeper connection with God.

Finally, in section 4, loving others as ourselves, we'll shift the focus from our inward, individual bodies as temples, to the outward—the body of Christ. We'll explore how confession, forgiveness, and simplicity transform not only our personal lives but also our relationships with God, others, and the world. Rooted in our identity through the Trinity, we're called to live in connection, not isolation. By letting go of burdens, we create space for God's grace to flow through us, connecting us with His purpose. As we humbly confront what weighs us down and offer it to Him, we find freedom, healing, and the strength to move our focus from ourselves to loving and serving others in His name.

Each chapter is intended to be completed over a week. By the time you finish this 12-week program, you'll be able to identify and track the daily and weekly activities that bring you closer to knowing and experiencing God's beauty and presence. You'll also be equipped to observe and adjust how you spend your time and the things you think about so you can have maximum impact.

Bear in mind that the weekly exercises are meant to bring you freedom, not the opposite. If you begin to feel encumbered by the activities, take a rest from the 12-week program and pick it back up when you're ready.

Learning to live and move and exist in God (Acts 17:28) will be a unique experience to each of us. The intent of this book is to discover something fun and new and feel the effects from activities that become meaningful rituals. Some will stick, and others that you initially disregard may meet you where you are in the future. The goal is to enrich your life and understand yourself better so that you can better understand those around you. And in turn, you'll help to enrich their lives in the way God intends.

Give yourself permission to abandon what you think you know and embrace the possibility of what God has uniquely planned for you—things you haven't even begun to imagine. When you do, you'll open the door to blessings and opportunities far greater than anything you could have dreamed—gifts that only God can present to you. If you're ready to fall down that

INTRODUCTION

rabbit hole, then this is the book for you. Rest assured that the man, the teacher, our God and Creator, Jesus, is waiting there for you.

And here is my prayer for all who follow Jesus. I encourage each of us to not put God in a container. The wonders of this world that He created and gave to us are worth lingering our thoughts and hearts on. Those wonders make it worth wandering down the path to new activities or reading materials that we may have written off for one reason or another in the past. And in the process, we may stumble across some of the most gratifying and meaningful aspects of life truly lived. And we may also find the most entertaining friendships with the people we least expect.

By turning our palms up and closing our eyes, we'll invite the Holy Spirit to transform every part of our person: heart, mind, and soul. I am confident your relationship with Him will grow in unimaginable ways. Your relationship with yourself and others will become less strained and frustrating and require less time and energy. And you will blossom and bear the fruit of the Holy Spirit in the form of *"love, joy, peace, patience, kindness, goodness, faithfulness, gentleness, and self-control"* (Galatians 5:22–23a).

So are you ready to take a step through the looking glass?

> *"I am the LORD your God, who teaches you what is best for you, who directs you in the way you should go."*
> —Isaiah 48:17 NIV

SECTION 1:

"Love the Lord Your God with All Your Heart"

CHAPTER 1:
THE ART AND SCIENCE OF US

For the Spirit of God has made me, and the breath of the Almighty gives me life.

—Job 33:4

In the mid-1800s, naturalist writer Henry David Thoreau lived in simplicity and solitude for over two years. Secluded in his friend Ralph Waldo Emerson's cabin in Massachusetts, Thoreau pondered the things of life on Walden Pond and recorded his poetic and reflective findings.[4]

On Walden Pond, Thoreau isolates himself from people, the progress of culture, materialism, and the idea of more. Instead he prioritizes the simplification of lifestyle by being in nature. He muses on man, as in humanity, as part of nature; and comes to understand that we have sacred ties to it. He reflects on our bodies as our temples. He meditates. And he recognizes that improvement of life occurs not outside ourselves but within.

I read *Walden* while separating myself from everyday life during my shingles episode, and it spoke to my soul. Thoreau wrote a personal collection of observations that combined both mindfulness and science, which became for him a spiritual experience. There are moments in our lives when the things that truly matter begin to enlarge. Getting into nature seems to do the trick for many of us. We turn off life's hurry by going for a hike and looking out over a summit, we stare up at the stars, or take in a sunrise. The worry and bitterness of life falls off, and we can feel into the sweet cherry center of it. In that moment, our eyes become like those of an innocent child. And somehow, we also gain the perspective of someone who has only months to live—that life is short and that we better make the most of it while we have the chance.

On the other hand, there are also times when days turn into weeks and months into years, until one day it dawns on us that we feel stagnant, aimless, uninspired. We want to feel alive again, but we can't kickstart it.

The truth is we come alive when we are connected to our Creator. And we connect to Him by paying attention to what He's done, how He's doing it, and what we think He'll do next. We are often so caught up in our own things that our minds don't allow us to look behind the veil of our everyday experience. And displayed on the other side of that veil are God's scientific and artistic creations. Taking a few minutes each day to bathe in their beauty connects us to ourselves and connects us to our Creator. Whether you believe in God or not, it's easy to see that our world is a work of art. All you have to do is look up at the sky, get lost in the architecture of a rose, or consider how your body operates without your conscious awareness. And as a Christian, I'm overcome with awe that behind it all is a master artist in whose image we humans are made.

God's Ultimate Masterpiece

The natural world around us reflects God's creativity, wisdom, and goodness; in it, all the attributes of an invisible God are made visible. And His guidance can be discerned through the order and beauty found within the creation—guidance that you can hold and squeeze and touch and know. Guidance that can still the distress and storms around you. Guidance that fills your body and soul with enthusiasm, confidence, courage, and fearlessness. How do you get this guidance? By being willing to step back from your current state of mind and make space for what God wants you to think about and see.

In this book, you'll discover tools to help remove the veil, which will allow the eyes of your heart to shift. And that shift begins by focusing first on His favorite thing: us.

We are the ultimate masterpiece in God's six-day creation project: *"God formed man from the dust of the ground. He breathed the breath of life into the man's nostrils and the man became a living person"* (Genesis 2:7). God's breath of life, or the Hebrew translation for breath, *ruakh*, which means Spirit, made us alive!

And then we were empowered to join Him in co-creation. In the words of King David:

> *You made all the delicate, inner parts of my body and knit me together in my mother's womb. Thank you for making me so wonderfully complex! Your*

workmanship is marvelous—how well I know it. You watched me as I was being formed in utter seclusion, as I was woven together in the dark of the womb. You saw me before I was born. Every day of my life was recorded in your book. Every moment was laid out before a single day had passed.
—Psalm 139:13–16

The Lord says, "*I will guide you along the best pathway for your life. I will advise you and watch over you*" (Psalm 32:8).

The dimensions of a person—mind, heart, soul, and spirit—are contained within the domain of our body, or as philosopher and theologian Dallas Willard calls it, "our little power pack."[5] He emphasized the integral role of our physical body as the power pack God has assigned us in shaping our actions, freedom, and overall growth. And my friends, that is the pervasive idea that inspired the framework of this book.

Our Body Is Our Temple

To grasp the fact that the Spirit of God made us, we need look no further than the concept that Thoreau considered: Our body is our temple. That is, our emotional and physical well-being correlate with the body as a Temple for Christ.

We followers of Jesus speak a lot about connecting to God through our minds and through our hearts and our souls. But we mostly ignore our physical body and its connection to God. Our power pack, however, is so important to God that He tells us that our bodies are not only temples, but they are also where the Spirit of God makes His home (1 Corinthians 3:16–17).

First Corinthians 6:20 says plainly, *"You must honor God with your body."*

Approaching the care and appreciation of our bodies with reverence, tenderness, and empathy is essential. It's like taking care of a plant that needs nurturing and protection. Or maybe you're like me and don't have a green thumb, but you have raised a teenager and learned to show gentleness and understanding to him instead of reacting aggressively. It's not only important to treat our loved ones with tenderness and understanding, but to extend the same care to ourselves.

Caring for the body goes beyond not ingesting toxic things or making poor choices with our bodies. At the root, it's about what we think about ourselves, our mindset toward ourselves. We are so good at wasting thought energy tearing ourselves down through negativity and tearing our bodies down through self-criticism. But God guides us back to what we should think about ourselves: His workmanship is marvelous. Remember that how we think about our physical body is how we think about our whole self.

Fortunately, you can train yourself, like I have, to be in constant awe of your body's sophisticated workings. I didn't get to this place on my own. My mom Valerie would not let me get away with one negative thought about my teenage body. If I mentioned my cankles in front of her, she responded with, "What are you talking about? Your legs are strong and beautiful!" Later in life, when I showed her how small my chest had gotten after nursing two children, she jumped in with, "They are shaped beautifully, and you'll see, they will grow and change a lot in the next few years!" We all could use a Val in our lives. If you don't have one, you can practice hearing the voice of our Creator saying in effect: "Knock it off with those negative thoughts and put my thoughts in you. Marvel at the complexity of your body and the work of art that you are."

And if God's Word isn't enough to inculcate the truth that our bodies are sacred vessels, He put some skin in the game. A physical body was the means by which the God of the heavens embodied Himself on earth—through the birth of Jesus from Mary. Like all humans, only in connection to His mother Mary, through the umbilical cord, did He breathe.

Whether people loved Him, were shocked by Him, or despised Him, Jesus grew into a man that they were eager to meet, hear from, and know more about. He healed sick people by physically touching them or by His mere words. Jesus breathed his last breath in our natural world while hanging on a cross. But by supernatural means He breathed again—fully alive and glorified. In this perfect bodily state He ascended back to where He came from. But to ensure that we are never alone, He left us with the gift of the Holy Spirit.

Our body is our temple, and it's where that invisible Spirit of God, makes His home. When we're in a dark place and feeling low, connecting to God is the most important thing we can do, especially when we're at our end and need help. He promises to never leave us. And when we come to trust that promise, we begin to see and know Him whether our days are dark, dull, or bright. The Spirit of God is magnificent power. It gives us hope and inspires us to live our fullest life now, not just in the afterlife. It's a power that helps us embrace each day with purpose and visible action.

God Breathes – We Breathe

Henry David Thoreau had to remove himself from the noise of the world to gain perspective on what really matters. He immersed himself in the quiet power of nature for two whole years. That's certainly one way to do it. In the same way, we can sucker punch our feelings of aimlessness and focus on what matters by allowing God to guide us into simplicity. Simplicity is found in rest, and rest can be accessed by our breath.

God's breath gives us ours. *"He breathed into his nostrils the breath of life, and the man became a living being"* (Genesis 2:7b). The Hebrew word that we mostly see for "breath" in the Old Testament is *ruakh*. It has several meanings in the Biblical Hebrew. One is "wind," and one is "spirit" as in, "the spirit of humanity; an intellectual frame of mind." The third meaning we see is "breath" that supports life or life force.

In Genesis 2:7b, the spotlight is on God. It's His breath that gives life to the man. Until God takes the initiative, the man is completely lifeless. This shows that life itself is directly connected to God's breath, His spirit. Every moment of our existence depends on Him, and when He chooses to withdraw that breath, our physical bodies return to dust. We are helpless.

One of my favorite images of this is in Ezekiel 37:5b–6, where God breathes life into dry bones:

> *I am going to put breath into you and make you live again. I will put flesh and muscles on you and cover you with skin. I will put breath into you, and you will come to life. Then you will know that I am the* Lord.

And then, just as He says, it happens! It's such a powerful picture of God's ability to bring life, hope, and restoration to even the most hopeless situations.

Ruakh in both these verses implies both literal breathing and life force or spirit. We are made up of physical bodies and intangible life force or spirit. Air, a mixture of created elements, connects us to God and to the world we live in. It's invisible yet visible. We can breathe on a mirror and although we don't see the breath leaving us, we can see its foggy mark and even use our index finger to draw a picture in it.

God has chosen to breathe into you just as you are. We can remember God's power in our own breath, and meditating on that can bring us to a state of rest. So let's get right to it and practice that.

Restful Breath Exercise

Sit comfortably with a tall, lengthened spine. Relax your shoulders and place your hands on your knees, palms up. Close your eyes gently. Inhale through your nose and then exhale through your nose for a little longer than the inhale. Begin by counting to four on the inhale, then exhale for a count of four. Do that again, inhaling for four, then exhaling for five this time. Inhale for four, then exhale for six. And again, all the way up to exhaling for eight.

While doing this, relax your jawbone, your hands, your face, your shoulders. Simply breathe.

Slow controlled breathing brings our nervous system to a place of rest. From that place, we can think more clearly. The eyes of our heart can begin to open and see that the vessel of our body is sacred. It's a gift. And we begin to feel alive.

When practicing controlled breathing exercises, many people mistakenly separate the body's physiological response from awareness of our Creator. We must recognize that He designed us in this unique way. Why shouldn't we make the most of our unique design? He did not leave us without tools to give our minds and bodies rest. From this lens, breath work can be a spiritual exercise, an act of worship. It can create space inside for God's presence to be known.

I didn't know the power of these exercises until my early twenties. And the biggest hurdle to getting there was giving myself permission to experience them. Let me take you back to my early days to explain this.

Quieting Ourselves

Body awareness, coordination, and movement have always gotten my juices flowing. My parents signed me up for gymnastics at the age of four, and it was the perfect outlet for my nonstop energy. I'm grateful for their support in helping me find a way to express myself. I competed for years, but at age twelve, they shifted me to dance classes when my hips and curves grew in. In high school, I loved cheerleading, and I became passionate about group fitness classes, eventually becoming an instructor. It was all intense physical stuff.

After college, I moved to Macau, a former Portuguese colony known as the Vegas of China. It was a beautiful blend of cultures, from the architecture and food to the faces of the people. With my degree in hand, I joined a small team to teach English to Chinese and Brazilian adults. The team was planting a church, led by Pastor Mark, an American from Indiana, and a linguistic wonder, fluent in many Chinese dialects.

One day, a student invited me to a Qi Gong session. Despite having only tried a single yoga class at a gym in Southern California, an awful one, at that, I agreed to the new experience. As I watched the group in the dimly lit room, I couldn't help but feel a sense of awe. Each person moved in their own unique way, all in deep focus, breathing slowly and deliberately. The energy in the room was palpable, and I couldn't help but feel inspired by the collective sense of mindfulness and presence. It was a powerful reminder of the beauty and power of being fully present in the moment.

The next day, I had a conversation with Pastor Mark to better understand what I had seen. He did not criticize or judge, but instead shared an insightful perspective. He explained that there is an intangible force that surrounds us, and by practicing techniques like massage, acupuncture, martial arts, meditation, or Tai Chi, we can harness this energy to enhance our well-being. Qi Gong, for instance, utilizes breath, movement, and intention to promote balance and vitality within our bodies. His insights taught me to keep an open mind, step out of my comfort zone, and not limit myself to what is visible. It was a life-changing experience that helped me realize the importance of channeling inner energy through less intense, more subtle physical movement to create a positive outlook on life. I learned that when I quieted myself, my inner guide got louder; that inner guide is the voice of the Holy Spirit.

Our bodies are magnificent units that combine science, art, and poetry. Let's journey further into appreciating the body's unique design, but this time we'll wear the hat of a scientist. So put on your lab coat.

Actions and Reactions

Our body is complex and made up of many systems that operate independently but also as part of the whole. Think about some of your body's systems for a moment: endocrine, digestive, reproductive, nervous, respiratory, muscular, circulatory, skeletal, lymphatic, and more. And all these systems operate without our conscious awareness. What's more, our whole existence relies on elements in nature, essential materials like water and air. We can't make water, and we can't make air. Human beings are a part of the collective phenomenon of nature.

Let's go even deeper under the microscope. Our bodies run on chemical energy, which we obtain from carbohydrates, proteins, and fats. That energy is then converted into different forms, such as thermal, kinetic, and chemical energy, in a process called energy metabolism. Ultimately, that energy comes from the sun to fuel all life on earth. Scientists recognize that everything in the universe is made of energy, including us. Energy powers our world, and it powers us.

Despite being invisible to the naked eye, the effects of these energetic processes are very visible. It's fascinating to consider how these actions and reactions are interconnected. It's even more fascinating to consider how invisible, God-created power and energy within us can be harnessed in incredible ways. How we choose to manage and use this God-given energy makes a difference. It impacts not only ourselves but also those closest to us and even the strangers we encounter throughout the day. And those seemingly small and inane interactions are what change our world for the better.

I was inspired recently by the perseverance and positive attitude of an elderly woman I met on a nearby walking trail. I could sense her tenacity as she hobbled along. It was like you could hear the air around her speak joyfulness. After a short greeting, I learned that she had been living with MS for most of her life. She chose to keep moving. MS did not break her. I also learned that she was a believer. The rewards for her staying close to God no matter the terrain or distance she faced brought her a peace beyond anything this world could give.

The story of the elderly woman could be any of ours. Our setbacks often serve as setups for God to reveal His incredible power. When we feel backed into a corner, that's often the moment we witness His best work. No matter the challenges we face, God's plan for our lives remains steady and unshaken. Through our struggles, He shapes us, making us more humble, compassionate, and understanding toward others. And there's no greater joy than watching His plan rise above our circumstances, turning difficulties into something beautiful. And we can take comfort in knowing that God is the one who fights for us. Our role, He says, is to return to him, rest in Him, and find strength in quietness and confidence (Isaiah 30:15). In this way, we allow God to move within us and clearly see how He is moving around us.

Recap

There is a connection between our physical health and the guide who lives in our hearts. Our physical well-being along with our emotional, mental, and spiritual well-being comes down to how we play our part in the energetic world. We have personal choices when it comes to what we do to and with our bodies. And the more we stay connected to God, the more He can use us as a conduit for His good and His purpose for us in this world. We get aligned with His guidance for us by making space for Him by noticing the beauty around us and especially in our own body's unique design. Taking a few minutes each day to bathe in that beauty connects us to ourselves and to our Creator.

Those who take care of their physical well-being by treating their bodies with kindness and self-control are easy to spot. Eating healthy foods, consciously breathing, exercising, and sleeping well are some of the ways to do this. When we live in this way, we feel better. When we feel better, we think better thoughts. And when our mind and outlook are in a good place, we are partnering with God to create an environment for Him to work through. Therefore, our physical bodies play a spiritual role in our world. Through nurturing all the parts of our person—mind, body, spirit, and soul—we have the potential to tap into the unlimited resources of God.

Well that's it for this week. Next week we'll dive further into the four areas in which to honor our temple bodies: body mindset, food, exercise, and rest. Let's get to this week's activities.

Activities Week 1

Heart (physical exercise): Walk outside, in nature if you can, for ten to fifteen minutes each day this week. Share the activity with a spouse or go alone—no earbuds, no music. Rain or shine, commit to doing it. Log it in your journal or on a piece of paper.

Mind (cleanse): Practice the restful breath exercise each morning this week.

Soul (renew and restore): Create space for good sleep: This week, ensure you are asleep by ten each night. By that time, make sure you have done whatever you need to do to complete your day and be ready to welcome relaxation: kitchen cleaned phone on silent and set aside, showered or bathed—whatever that routine is for you. The time for shut-eye is ten o'clock.

Love Your Neighbor (scripture and prayer): Read Psalm 139 out loud each morning this week. Pray thanks; ask for help and guidance; and pray for God's power to enter your circumstance.

CHAPTER 2:
TEMPLE BODY POWER

It is through the body that we are related to one another and to the rest of the world.

—Mihaly Csikzentmihalyi

Let's pretend we're taking a walk around the globe between 700 and 900 BC. Cue the stringed instruments.

We'll begin in Greece 776 BC, the first Olympic Games on record are being held in Olympia as a festival to honor and worship Zeus and the other gods. The Olympics were a religion to the ancient Greeks; an Olympic participant at the peak of their athleticism was immortalized. On the third night of the five-day games, we watch as everyone marches in procession to the temples of Zeus and Hera and other shrines to offer prayers and sacrifices.

Meanwhile further east, in India between 700 BC and 900 BC, the Brahmanas and Upanishads are being composed as part of the Vedas centered around a collection of hymns and poems.

These are the texts that provide the ritual and philosophical foundation for Hinduism. Yoga first appears here.

Now we time travel forward from the BCs to around AD 50, and we're in Greece again, specifically Corinth, and we're reading one of the letters that the Apostle Paul wrote to a church there. In it, he challenges the Corinthians: *"Do you not know that your bodies are temples of the Holy Spirit, who is in you, whom you have received from God? You are not your own; you were bought at a price. Therefore honor God with your bodies"* (1 Corinthians 6:19–20 NIV).

Imagine if everywhere you went—your office in the morning, lunch or afternoon meetings, home in the evening—you were aware that you are carrying God inside you, in your body. Everywhere you walk throughout the day, you are a mobile temple of God. Every encounter would be a chance for anyone you meet to know more about not *what* you carry within you but *who*. Would you do anything differently? Stand differently? Converse or act differently toward the people who cross your paths? Would you think different thoughts about yourself, about others? If so, the impact on your own life and the lives of those around you and the world beyond would be unimaginable. Being aware that you are carrying God's power within your temple body would change the world.

Throughout the Bible, it's very clear that God values our bodies, and the New Testament teaches that being good stewards of our temple body has a lot of leeway. We are given nothing but absolute freedom in what we do to and with our body. We are alive in Christ. But with this freedom comes a call to use it wisely: to honor God, ourselves, and others through our actions. This is no small challenge; our human nature often pushes us toward doing whatever we want without considering responsibilities or consequences. Yet, embracing the awareness of God's presence within us invites us to rise above that nature, living intentionally and with purpose. We are called to live as His ambassadors in the world.

Let's explore four areas in which we can honor our temple bodies: body mindset, food, exercise, and rest.

Honoring Our Temple Body with a Body Mindset

What fills your thoughts most of the time? Take a moment.

Is it money, work, your kids? What if I told you that God actually instructed us on how He wants us to think about all things—even our bodies: *"Brothers and sisters, whatever is true, whatever is honorable, whatever is just, whatever is pure, whatever is lovely, whatever is commendable, if there is any excellence, if there is anything worthy of praise, think about these things"* (Philippians 4:8 ESV).

In terms of your body, this instruction to cultivate positive, high-frequency thinking reveals how God sees us. By understanding His perspective and thoughts about us, we can begin to view ourselves in the same way. Think about the implications of that. God invites us to move away from the negativity that so often feels automatic and instead flip that switch into a powerful, positive thought frequency rooted in His truth.

Yes, it means when you look in the mirror, you're aware of your strong legs carrying you through your day, your hands for doing the work you've asked of them. You recognize that your five senses are fully functioning, bringing color and richness to life. Ladies, you honor your endocrine system for its monthly rhythms, or that you grew a baby inside you at some point in your life. Or maybe you're thankful that your digestive system is working as it should and that your immune system is boosted and operating well. Maybe you're marveling at the coordination of all those systems working without you putting any mental effort into it. Be in awe at your body for the gift that it is.

But the Philippians passage points us to so much more than that. It's not just about appreciating your physical self; it's about making Christlike, high-frequency choices daily to honor yourself and others, because Jesus knows you're capable. And here's the extraordinary truth: He doesn't just want more for you than you even want for yourself. No. He's ready to give you more than you could even imagine for yourself.

Let's go to another important topic that affects our body mindset. I can't write a book about our temple bodies and how we relate to them without mentioning the most powerful carnal feeling we have as humans: our sexual life. So we're going there.

Concerning our sexual lives we read this in 1 Corinthians 6:12: *"'I have the right to do anything' you say—but not everything is beneficial"* (NIV). In this verse, commentators believe that Paul may be echoing a common saying by Christians at the time. Maybe they were gloating and saying, "I'm free to live the ways of hedonistic Roman culture because I'm saved by my belief that Jesus Christ is Messiah." Paul wants them to know that salvation doesn't work like that.

Desire is strong in each of us, and our sexual desire is one of the best ways to understand how powerful desire can be. Sex—done in love, commitment, and covenant—is transcendent. You lose yourselves in nothing but feeling with one another; your minds shut down, and you easily surrender yourself to the other person. Through physical pleasure, your souls connect. Life is created through the sexual union.

Sexual Temptations

But like anything, we as humans are so good at distorting sexual desire. Remember, *"Everything is permissible, but not everything is beneficial"* (1 Corinthians 10:23 CSB). Consider this example:

> A man bored with his marriage of fifteen years, though he still loves her, lusts after another woman in their friend group. The other woman picks up on this attention and decides there is something there—something that might feel better than the life she and her husband have created. After all, she thinks to herself: My husband and I have spent years struggling with our finances, and this other man makes a lot of money. The man thinks to himself: I've been bored with my wife for years. I've ached for sexual intimacy, and she's busy running the kids around and doesn't make me a priority. They don't resist the temptation and finally indulge. What started as a secret is made known, and two families are shattered. The ripple effect spreads beyond the nuclear family to the extended family, their friends, their workplaces, and their own futures.

I wonder what the outcome would have been if, when the man faced temptation, he had spent some time hearing from wives and kids of cheating husbands. Maybe his heart would have been stirred to make very different choices that would not have broken two families.

Sex before commitment can carry a significant mental and emotional weight for anyone. Here's why: Sex magically covers over things that might bother us. In a marriage, it works like a charm in quelling issues or frustrations from unnecessarily escalating into bigger problems. But outside of commitment, sex can obscure serious red flags. Two people who are well-matched in this arena may find themselves ignoring deeper incompatibilities. What could have been a brief connection or a few casual dates can turn into a strained relationship, one that feels forced as you struggle to make it work. You want the relationship to fall into place so badly, but it doesn't.

God desires peace within ourselves and within our relationships. When our thoughts are filled with confusion, anxiety, or the strain of trying to force something, that peace is disrupted. We end up feeling lost, confused, and unsure of the direction to take.

The full gift of intimacy through sex as God intended for us, and the physical act of sex are two very different things. Having been married for two decades, this I know. Two individuals dealing with their own difficulties, stumbling through life, continue to grow and guard their marriage by it. And sex can be seen as a barometer for how the marriage is doing. Are you respecting, serving, honoring, and loving *each other* well outside the bedroom? That will show up in the bedroom. And are you respecting, serving, honoring, and loving *yourself* outside the bedroom? That will show up in the bedroom too.

And I can think of no better way to follow this discussion of sexual intimacy than moving on to food.

Honoring Our Temple Body with Food

"You are what you eat" rings just as true today as it did in the past. I like to keep food choices simple in my family: Take in whole food in moderate portions, and our body's systems will have the best chance of operating at their optimal level. I consider whole foods those found around the perimeter of the supermarkets, which is an idea I first heard about when reading about the "Zone Diet" as we called it in the late1990s.[6] Take in too much of the wrong foods, those that are processed and high in sugar, and potential diseases begin to mound up.

Combatting Americans' lack of focus on the link between having good health and eating whole food is an uphill battle. For many reasons, we have not done a great job of connecting food to good health as other cultures have.

When I lived in China, this was one of the features of their culture that immediately had my heart. The idea of food, herbs, and spices as medicine and something that keeps us in step with the natural rhythms of our world was novel. Yet, it seemed so intuitive. For the Chinese, it wasn't just about eating for weight management or to compliment training for a sport like weightlifting or long-distance running. Up to that point that had been mostly how I viewed my dietary regimen.

The fast food and processed food industry has its grip on America. The increase in diseases and the pills or surgeries to help fight these ills have moved in lockstep with the increase in obesity. Even though these facts are known, this is not enough for many Americans to decrease their consumption of processed foods, which is the path of least resistance. And our hectic American lifestyle makes the drive-through at fast food restaurants so convenient.

As with anything that requires change, it starts at the individual level. It begins with a spark in our intent and will, which leads to making small changes to our thought patterns and acting on those thoughts throughout our day. That's where good habits begin. Then comes the impact. We all know people who have lost weight and kept it off for good. That is one of the hardest things to do, but the freedom we see in these people after their goals are met is astounding. They are no longer slaves to what once was their master.

And I don't mean to write about food and nutrition cavalierly. I may sound like I'm oversimplifying. It's just that we are on information overload. Should we be keto, vegetarian, vegan, carnivore, eat for our body type, eat for our blood type? Should we do intermittent fasting? The amount of time and energy that people spend thinking about issues related to food intake can be draining. Unhappiness about our body types, wishing we looked like someone else, obsessing over our clothes fitting more loosely, or despondency for failing to stick with a diet is hurting us. And I've found that when things get overwhelming, less is more.

Speaking of less—when it comes to food: fasting. That is a topic I'm passionate about; I'll dive into it in a later chapter. But for now, consider the following advice. By whatever authority I have in sharing this, here I go:

> Be released from your prior food mistakes and guilt. Start anew. Put 80 percent great things into your body each week: fruits, vegetables, meats, and healthy grains. The rest of the time, eat a cookie or two that your kids just baked. And start now. Don't wait for "next Monday" or "after the holiday." You'll just keep waiting. Do what you tell your kids: Make good choices. And enjoy living your life each day.

Honoring Our Temple Body with Exercise

The third way to honor our temple bodies centers around healthy movement. The root word for "exercise" is the Latin term *exercere*, which is made up of "ex" meaning "out" and "arcere" meaning "to keep in." The term has a fascinating feel about it. The original sense of the word was not just about engaging in some form of activity, but in maintaining readiness or skill. Its essence is to practice, work at, develop, and continue moving.

In Bible times people mostly traveled by foot. While there aren't exact records of daily distances walked, estimates suggest that people in the ancient Mediterranean world often walked between ten to twenty miles per day when traveling. The concept of exercise for the average person wasn't a thing back then, other than for warriors training for the sake of their nation or athletes training for sporting events. And it's worth mentioning, what was grown from the ground or raised in the fields was what they took in for food.

While the Bible doesn't explicitly prescribe specific exercises for our bodies, it has plenty to say about the importance of training. It draws parallels between physical discipline and the spiritual discipline required to grow in faith, resilience, and purpose. First Corinthians 9:24–27 tells us:

> *Don't you realize that in a race everyone runs, but only one person gets the prize? So run to win! All athletes are disciplined in their training. They do it to win a prize that will fade away, but we do it for an eternal prize. So I run with purpose in every step. I am not just shadowboxing. I discipline my body like an athlete, training it to do what it should.*

Let's take a closer look at the Roman world Paul lived in when he wrote these words. To the Ancient Greeks, athleticism and heroism were sacred, revered as godlike qualities. The Olympics weren't just sporting events; they were religious ceremonies. What started as a simple footrace grew into competitions like javelin, discus, wrestling, and boxing, all rooted in the mythology and paganism of Greek culture.

When the Romans conquered Greece in the second century BC, they redefined the games and infused them with spectacle and violence. Enter the gladiators. Yet, even in this evolution, the connection between athletics and religion remained.

Athletes trained relentlessly, driven by the promise of a crown, which was the ultimate symbol of honor and achievement. These men (women were excluded) were celebrated as heroes, wielded as political tools, and idolized throughout the Mediterranean. But for all their fame and glory, their victories and prizes were fleeting, destined to fade with time.

Paul flips this imagery, calling us to pursue a prize that doesn't fade: a life rooted in God, eternal and unshakable. He challenges us to live with the same dedication and purpose as those athletes, but for a crown that endures forever.

Honoring our temple bodies starts with physical activity, doing what makes us feel strong and alive. But Paul's message goes beyond exercise. The idea of running to win is a call to live intentionally, with commitment, not with half-hearted effort. It's about showing up daily, sometimes with baby steps, other times with bold leaps, but always moving forward. Each step strengthens us spiritually, drawing us closer to God. The ultimate prize? Fulfillment that lasts forever. So run with purpose in every step, pursuing the eternal reward only God can give.

Training Our Energy

Our home sits at the bottom of a hill in Northern California, surrounded by the breathtaking beauty of what truly feels like God's country. We live in a valley framed by the majestic Cascade Mountains, with stunning views of both Mount Shasta and Mount Lassen. When our kids give us attitude, we send them outside to run up and down the hill a few times. When our kids were babies and filled with non-specific angst, we would take them outside to get a change of scenery and sensations. The crying would cease. When they were toddlers, we'd have them "get their wiggles out" before we sat them down to concentrate on a task.

I have news. We are no different as adults. We all carry energy in our bodies. Moving our bodies and paying attention to our breathing is how we can begin to shift our mindset. Our energy must be funneled into a physical activity for our overall well-being whether it be walking, swimming, cycling, yoga, pickle ball, basketball, Pilates, weightlifting, or whatever you enjoy. We cannot run a metaphorical race that lasts through all eternity without addressing our physical body and its energy.

Our culture is one that sits, not one that averages walking twenty miles per day. When we choose to sit and do nothing with that energy, over time our bodies will oblige. In fact, our bodies will continue to do *more* nothing with that energy until the energy is impotent.

Johns Hopkins lists the health risks linked to a sedentary lifestyle, which include: the development of high blood pressure, an increased risk of Type 2 diabetes, increased likelihood of developing coronary heart disease, more anxiety and depression, and an increase in certain cancers.[7]

What does the Bible say we do with our energy in modern times? Ours is a time when mental health issues are high, when people are more sedentary than ever, and when people are feeling confused about so many things in the world.

Dr. Curt Thompson, a psychiatrist and follower of Jesus, who focuses on interpersonal neurobiology, wrote this in *Anatomy of the Soul*: "Movement exercises like yoga and tai chi can enhance awareness of your body's sensations and breathing. They can put you at ease so that you're able to respond to stress more easily."[8] Dr. Thompson describes the triad of neuroplasticity in our brains, which are made up of new neurons, new neuron connections, and pruning neurons (those which are no longer needed). He explains that these neurons are created first, by aerobic exercises; second, by focused attention exercises (like meditation); and third, by novel learning experiences (taking that painting class you've always wanted to). By moving our bodies in big ways, small ways, loud ways, or quiet ways, we can nurture a calm state within ourselves.

Yoga and the Yoke of Jesus

According to the website yogaearth.com, approximately 300 million people around the world regularly practice yoga. It's reported that around 36 million Americans practice yoga. One in three Americans have tried it at least once. Yoga continues to be a growing trend as measured by search queries on Google and the value of the yoga industry's annual growth.[9]

Yoga is a controversial topic for many Jesus followers. I'll dive more deeply into this controversy in chapter 6. My intent is to help Christians understand this ancient technique that is known to improve our mental, emotional, and physical well-being and to help maybe-believers understand the conflict. Allow me to walk you through my introduction to yoga.

The first time I truly embraced yoga was nearly twenty-five years ago while serving as a Korean linguist in the Army. Our military base sat at the top of a massive, perpetually fog-covered hill in Monterey, California, but as you made your way down the hill, whether on foot or by car, the sun would break through. We were surrounded by high-end restaurants, boutique shops, and the endless horizon of the ocean. Nestled in this picturesque scene was a yoga studio called "Yoga Sanctuary." I could never have dreamed up a more appropriate name.

Each week, I'd walk into my hot yoga class carrying the mental and emotional weight that came with being an active-duty soldier. I felt the strain of military life, the pressure of looming language exams, the constant institutional grind, and the irrational demands from sergeants. But ninety minutes later, I'd walk out sweaty but with an entirely new perspective.

I would feel gratitude for the opportunity to serve my country and more connected with those who served decades and centuries before me. I felt a sense of ownership over the beautiful free nation we get to live, grow, and thrive in. And on a more personal level, I felt hope for what lay ahead after my time in the Army, particularly a future with Adam, the Airman I was dating then and who is now my husband of over twenty years. The contrast within my mind, body, and spirit before and after the yoga class could not have been more stark. In those moments, yoga became a sanctuary—not just a physical space but a practice that grounded me and connected all the parts of me when I needed it most.

In my experience, yoga offers much more than just physical exercise. It's a practice where I stretch, strengthen, and engage in an aerobic workout all at once. But beyond the physical benefits, yoga invites me into a space of silence, solitude, and stillness—an integration of both inward and outward spiritual disciplines, as defined by Richard Foster.[10] It's a time to step away from distractions, busyness, hurried schedules, demands, expectations, and the constant noise of life. Like a soldier training for battle, yoga helps me train *away* from anxiety, irritability, possessiveness, and resentment.

The word *yoga* means "to yoke." And yoke sounds like a really old reference, because it is. The *Collins Dictionary* defines "yoke" as a long piece of wood tied across the necks of two animals such as oxen, to make them walk close together when they are pulling a plow.[11] The oxen are tethered or "joined" together while being put to work. In this literal translation, the oxen are partnered for the single purpose of preparing the soil for planting seed, growth, and harvest. Similarly, in Sanskrit, the classical language of India and Hinduism, yoga or "to yoke" means to join, to unite, or to bind. So the yoga practice becomes a joining of mind, body, and spirit through the combination of focused attention, physical movements, and breath.

Jesus had something to say about His yoga or "yoke" in Matthew 11:28–30 (NIV):

> *Come to me, all you who are weary and burdened, and I will give you rest. Take my yoke upon you and learn from me, for I am gentle and humble in heart, and you will find rest for your souls. For my yoke is easy and my burden is light.*

By tethering ourselves to Jesus, conditions are right for our dirt to be dug into, broken up, and made ready to be planted. And He tells us that joining, uniting, and binding ourselves to Him is easy, light, and restful.

Letting Go of Resistance and Surrendering

In a yoga class, a student who holds her breath or pushes too hard builds up resistance, making the hour feel incredibly uncomfortable. The chances of her exploring yoga again as a physical activity are slim because she didn't get the results she wanted; it was too hard, and she didn't feel successful. In her struggle to force progress, she got in her own way, and resistance persisted.

But if she returns to class with the intention of giving herself time and space to breathe, then she's got some runway. By paying attention to her breath, she can become more aware of where resistance resides in her body. If she's holding her breath, it's a signal that she's gone too far in a pose. She needs to back off and find the sweet spot where she can fully exhale. That's where the process of letting go begins. That's where surrender happens.

This is a great metaphor for the life of one who resists learning about the Kingdom of Heaven. When they come with openness, ready to face the resistance within, they find rest. It's in turning away from the things of this world—what they've relied on, chased, and loved—that they discover the freedom to surrender their life to Jesus. It's not about forcing or striving; it's about letting go and finding peace in Him.

Honoring Our Temple Bodies with Rest

The Old Testament site called Brook Besor has come to be known as a place representing rest. But it didn't always. It started with King David and his 600 warriors. This was where they prepared for battle to get back something they had lost. Here is the story as recorded in 1 Samuel 30 (paraphrased):

King David's enemies, the Amalekites arrived at the town of Ziklag. They burned it and took all the people captive. Those people just so happened to be the wives and kids of King David and his men.

Three days after Ziklag had been destroyed, David and his men show up. They take in what's happened and cry until they can't anymore.

Then the mood shifts. Their sadness turns to anger. And it's directed at one person—their leader, David. They talk about stoning him, but David redirects things after getting supernatural strength from God. He brings in a priest to inquire of God *"Should I chase after this band of raiders? Will I catch them?"* And God answers him, *"Yes, go after them. You will surely recover everything that was taken from you!"* (1 Samuel 30:8). With that assurance, he moves.

David takes his 600 men to Brook Besor. But when they get there, 200 of those men hit a wall. They are exhausted and can go no further. Picture 200 of Mel Gibson/William Wallace's warriors in the movie *Braveheart* staying behind. They hear the speech: "They may take our lives, but they will never take our freedom!"[12] And 200 guys respond with, "You guys go ahead, we're gonna stay behind and rest. Be here when you get back!"

With no time to waste David and 400 men cross the ravine in hot pursuit. On the way forward, they run into an Egyptian slave of one of the Amalekites. His master had abandoned him. He turns out to be their golden ticket. He tells David everything that happened at Ziklag and obligingly leads them to their enemies.

When King David and his men come upon them, they are eating, drinking, reveling, and totally caught off guard. They fight from that evening until the next evening, and David's men get back everyone and everything that had been taken. They are reunited with their families, and it feels so good except that the anticipation of a different type of battle within David's army begins as they make their way back to Brook Besor.

Picture this: As David and his men approach, the 200 men who stayed behind finally see their wives and kids alive and well. David greets them, coming fresh off victory; there are smiles all around. But troublemakers in the bunch begin whining: *"They didn't go with us, so they can't have any of the plunder we recovered. Give them their wives and children, and tell them to be gone"* (1 Samuel 30:22). David responds:

> *No my brothers! Don't be selfish with what the LORD has given us. He has kept us safe and helped us defeat the band of raiders that attacked us. Who will listen when you talk like this? We share and share alike—those who go to battle and those who guard the equipment.*
> —1 Samuel 30:23–24

A profound thing worth mentioning is that the philosophy of King David's leadership shown here is still being used in military makeup today. Whether someone's role is "supply" or "infantry," they are all servant-hearted members serving in different ways for the good of the same team.

The Action-Rest Tension

David and his warriors were savage. And Brook Besor represents rest. Quite the paradox. God blesses both work and rest. He even taught us from the beginning of time to set aside one day a week for nothing but rest. For those 200 men to stay behind, they had to swallow some pride and admit exhaustion. Surrendering like that can be scary. It's uncomfortable. They risked disappointing the people around them. I'm sure they carried some serious guilt for not fighting alongside their brothers. They had to shrug off the shame of not doing what the others thought they should be doing, what they themselves expected to be doing: being a warrior and going hard at all costs.

I'm convinced it's only through God's wisdom and voice that we become attuned to the need to withdraw and say no. And it's through courage that we cross the line to make it so. When we create regular space in our day for rest, whatever rest means to each of us, we make space for not just our body, but our soul to rest. And our temple body becomes an environment for creativity to flow and perspective and attitudes to shift.

Together, the elements of rest, eating whole food, exercise, and having a positive body mindset lead to improved physical health, mental resilience, and a more fulfilling life. We're about to begin the final chapter in this section on loving God with all our heart. So far, we've narrowed in on moving our own bodies. Next, we'll pay attention to how and where God is moving. Before we do, let's begin practicing this week's activities.

Activities Week 2

Heart (physical exercise): Each morning this week, upon waking, go into the child's pose.[1] Walk your fingers up so your arms are stretched ahead of you. Everything is relaxed and sinking into the floor. Aim your hips back over your heels. Keep your knees

---

[1] If you are not familiar with the poses referenced in the weekly activities, you can find photos and how-to instructions at www.verywellfit.com. Simply click on the search icon and type in the pose name (e.g., "child's pose").

wide and relax your hip flexors. And breathe long deep breaths, keeping your jaw relaxed. Then simply walk your hands together in a prayer position, crossing the thumbs over gently.

Think these words of gratitude: "Thank you Lord that in your mercy you've restored my soul within me."[13] Stay in this posture for thirty seconds up to three minutes. We'll begin each day like this for the entire 12-week program.

Mind (cleanse): Do "Wake up, Shake up." Stand up. For twenty to thirty seconds, shake out each leg and foot, your hips, your arms and hands, and your head. Then hold your stance and breathe for a few breaths.

Soul (renew and restore): What activities do you enjoy? Think of an activity where you lose yourself and lose track of time. Is it drawing, painting, building, reading, crafting? Carve out fifteen minutes in your day to do that activity this week.

Loving Others (scripture and prayer): Read Psalm 23 and Matthew 11:28–30 each morning this week. Pray thanks; ask for help and guidance; and pray for God's power to enter your circumstance.

CHAPTER 3:
THE POWER OF INTENTION

The most terrifying thing is to accept oneself completely.
—Carl Jung

When my son was six years old, he stumbled upon an origami book that I had picked up on a whim in college. Whereas I never got past the crane, he intended to make every single piece. And he did. When he got to the complicated pieces toward the end of the book, he asked me to help him. It was one of those "helpless mom" moments. "Maybe we should see if Dad can help," I suggested. But my son stayed in it and then burned through two more origami books we got for him.

Our intentions combined with the discipline of practice are one powerful driving force.

We have plans and goals in life from the moment we hatch. Desire, which is natural instinct, is strong in all of us from babies nursing to eating solid foods, crawling to walking, teens clawing for independence, to love and marriage. As humans we like to set intentions to grow ourselves, make things grow, and watch things grow. Whether the goals are entrepreneurial; career-based; educational; service-oriented; following through on our ideas, hopes, and creations; or of a different nature like breaking through addictions or improving relationships, we intend to do what's on our hearts.

Let me ask you a question: If our desires, will, and intentions are that strong and if intent combined with commitment is that powerful of a force within the individual, what does that say about the intent and heart of the one who made us? What does it say about the one in whose image we are made—the one who calls us His children?

I'm convinced that our intentions and wills are a glimpse into God Himself. He has planned for each of us to live in this world at the perfect time and in the perfect place because He desires it. And He wants more for each of us than any of us can ever imagine. We discover what that is when we align our desires with His.

Let's Pretend . . .

You're making travel plans for an adventure. You'll be going by car to a new city. You have heard about the city but never been there though it has always been on your bucket list of places to visit. Just as Italy is known for its gondolas and waterways, Paris for its Eiffel Tower, and New York for its Statue of Liberty, you have heard that your destination city is designed like a magical kingdom—but better than Disneyland, they say. You've journeyed all day to get there, and now you've arrived.

But this city is different. People's lives are changed after experiencing it. Only one person can be in the city at a time. You know that no one except you will be entering it, and you know that it's safe to enter without a friend. You're not scared or disappointed to experience it alone, but you are a little nervous and excited. Besides, you're not the first person to go there. You selected and reserved your time slot online. This city has the highest ratings—it's five out of five stars on all its reviews. Your anticipation and expectations are high.

As you drive up to the entrance, the gate slowly opens at the center. Your eyes take it in, and it's as you heard it would be, but better. The city's rivers run clear like glass along each side of an enormous castle. You roll down the windows. The air tastes sweet and feels warm as you gaze upon gems in the water, but you realize it's just a reflection. You park your car under a canopy of shade from the vibrant green trees on either side of the road and slowly get out. You begin to walk toward the doors of the castle and notice that the walkway is lined on either side with perfectly spaced ancient olive trees. You feel more alive than ever before, and you hear a sound of motion ahead.

Just then, the doors to the castle open and out walks a radiant, beautiful person, emanating beauty and white light. The radiant person seems to glide more than walk, and their steps resonate with a rhythm that feels like it's syncing to your heartbeat. There's a serenity in their expression, a knowing smile that somehow eases your nerves. As they draw closer, you instinctively bow your head slightly, not out of fear, but out of reverence. Yet, before you can lower your gaze further, the figure raises a hand gently, motioning for you to look directly at them. You're surprised by the warmth in their eyes, which seem to hold the vastness of the universe and a deep, personal connection all at once.

"You've made it," the person says in a voice that's both powerful and tender, like the melody of all the perfect harmonies woven together. The sound seems to wrap around you, dissolving any trace of anxiety. "Welcome."

You want to speak, to ask questions, but it feels unnecessary. It's as if the figure already knows your thoughts, your exhilaration, and even your doubts. Instead, you let their words settle in your heart like a warm hug.

They extend a hand, inviting you to walk with them toward the castle doors, which now stand wide open. As you step forward, the air seems to hum with life. It's as if every leaf, every ripple in the river, and every stone on the path acknowledges your presence. You realize this isn't just a city; it's a place where every part of creation is alive, celebrating, and waiting for you to join in.

And then, the person kneels before you and looks up. They speak: "I know you, and you have my favor. I loved you before you were born and was there when you were knitted in your mother's womb. I'm so glad you have come. And I have a special task, assigned just for you. You are to . . ."

And like Neo visiting the Oracle in *The Matrix*, you hear a message for your ears only. Maybe you are to adopt a child, write a book or forgive someone who has wounded you or taken the most precious thing in your life from you. Or maybe you are to step out of comfort and into risk where you have everything to lose. Maybe it will mean leaping into the unfamiliar in a new vocation, leaving an abusive marriage, or taking the risk of staying in a marriage after a spouse cheats. Maybe you are to end a friendship or relationship or abstain from an addiction or add something to your life that you have always resisted. Or perhaps you're being asked to stay exactly where you are in your career, marriage, or family life—only you're asked to do so with a complete attitude and mental shift about your circumstance. Whatever you are being called into, it is unique to you; it's something big, maybe difficult, scary, or seemingly impossible.

Still kneeling, the person of light pulls out a baton like in a relay race and offers it to you. You are invited to grab hold of the other end. The baton dances like diamonds in front of your eyes.

"I can't do this. It's too much; I'm scared, and I don't really want to. I feel alone. If I do this, would you send someone to be with me, to help me do it? Who would that be?"

"My presence will go with you. You'll have everyone and everything you need. And I'll take it one step further. You'll feel rested while you accomplish what I ask of you," the radiant person says.

More fear and doubt creep in. "But what if your presence doesn't go with me? I'm not enough. I don't want to be on my own away from you and this place. Can you show me a little more so I can feel confident in taking this on? I need something more from you."

The person of light finally says, "I delight in you so much that I will show you more. Will you hold onto the other end of the baton?"

"Yes," you say sheepishly. You grab a hold, and then you feel an energy transferred to you and hear words that echo the reassurances of Ephesians 3:16–19:

> My glorious riches will strengthen you with power through my Spirit in your inner being. Then I can dwell in your heart through your faith. By being rooted and established in my love for you, you can have power together with all the other people who have come to visit me in this city and that I've sent out, to grasp how wide and long and high and deep is my love. And to know this love that surpasses knowledge, you can be filled to the measure of all my fullness.

And with that, you're ready. You take a step forward, your heart steady with anticipation. Hopeful. Open. Prepared to embrace the adventure of your assignment, knowing that every step ahead is guided by a purpose greater than you can imagine. The path glows with promise, and with each move forward, you feel more in step with the journey you were created to take.

The more we get to know God and spend time with Him, the more His desires become our desires. And His desire, intent, and plan for you is big, my friends.

Moses in the Rock

Now let's look at another person's journey to this place and see what assignment was waiting for him.

Moses had a similar experience to the one you just imagined. God's intention was for Moses to lead His chosen people, the

Israelites, out of slavery in Egypt and toward the land He had Promised them.

But Moses was nervous about grabbing hold of the baton, and responded to God like this:

> You've asked me to lead Your people, but You haven't told me who You're sending with me. Lord, You told me that You knew me by name and that I had found favor with You. Since You're pleased with me, teach me Your ways so I may know You and continue to find favor with You. Remember us; we are Your people.
>
> —Exodus 33:12–13, paraphrased

Then the Lord tells Moses that His presence will go with him and that He will give him rest (Exodus 33:14). But Moses is understandably scared. He keeps pleading with the Lord:

> If Your presence doesn't go with us, don't send me up from here. How will anyone know that You're pleased with me and Your people unless you go with us? What else will distinguish us from all the other people on the face of the earth?
>
> —Exodus 33:15–16, paraphrased

And the Lord obliges: *"I will do the very thing you have asked, because I am pleased with you and I know you by name"* (Exodus 33:17 NIV). But Moses is still scared. He then makes his big, bold, audacious, ask. Lord, he says, *"Show me your glory"* (Exodus 33:18 NIV). And this is where things get even more interesting.

We learn that God has body parts—a back, a face, hands, a voice. He also has a name. He's like you and me. He is not some nebulous entity of mere power and energy. The Lord says:

> *"I will make all my goodness pass before you, and I will call out my name, Yahweh, before you. For I will show mercy to anyone I choose, and I will show compassion to anyone I choose. But you may not look directly at my face, for no one may see me and live."* The LORD continued, *"Look, stand near me on this rock. As my glorious presence passes by, I will hide you in the crevice of the rock and cover you with my hand until I have passed by. Then I will remove my hand and let you see me from behind. But my face will not be seen."*
> —Exodus 33:19–23

With Moses's third request for reassurance, I picture God rolling His eyes. But here's what I realized: God waits for us. We think it's only the other way around, but He is patient. He is waiting for us to get past our insecurities and excuses to finally say yes to Him.

Prior to this part of Moses's story, he had had a laundry list of intimate experiences with God and had seen His immense power. Yet, he still doubted God's intent for him and felt insecure. Check out this list of encounters he experienced: the burning bush (Exodus 3:1–4:17), miracles and wonders before Pharaoh (Exodus 7:8–13), the ten plagues (Exodus 7:14–12:30), the Passover (Exodus 12:1–28), parting the Red Sea (Exodus 14:1–31), the pillar of fire at night and cloud by day to lead the Israelites in the desert (Exodus 13:21–22), the ten commandments given on Mount Sinai (Exodus 20), manna and quail to sustain them each day (Exodus 16:1–35), and God regularly spoke to Moses *"face to face as a man speaks to his friend"* (Exodus 33:11 ESV).

Despite all these experiences, Moses was still skeptical about God's power of intention for him. He still needed reassurance about what God was trying to do through him. Moses grabbed hold of the metaphorical baton, however, and said yes. He moved when it was time to move. And God was with him.

I can't move on from this story without pointing out one more thing. As God was planning to make all His goodness pass in front of Moses, He made a point of saying, *"And I will proclaim my name, the Lord, in your presence"* (Exodus 33:19 NIV).

So what's the big deal about God announcing His name? Here's a fun fact: Moses was the very first person to whom the God of Abraham, Isaac, and Joseph revealed His name, Yahweh. The first!

Think about your own name. It's more than just an identifier. It carries your personality forth, and your spirit somehow is embodied by it. We spend hours poring over potential names for our future children to find the perfect names. People know us by our names. Our past generations put a seal on us through our last names. And we show up for others when our names are called.

Yahweh not only revealed Himself to Moses by saying His own name, but He was offering him so much more. We learn, for example, that *"everyone who calls on the name of the* **Lord** ***will be saved"*** (Joel 2:32 emphasis added). And we learn that *"the name of the* Lord *is a strong tower; the righteous man runs into it and is safe"* (Proverbs 18:10 ESV, emphasis added). So through His name, we are saved, and we have a strong tower to run to and be kept safe.

What else do you have to offer us, Yahweh? The Lord might respond, "If you run to me, your tower and refuge, you'll find rest, and I'll send my angels to guard you" (Psalm 91:2, 11, paraphrased).

Got anything else to offer us in your name, Yahweh? "So glad you asked," He might respond and give this assurance as He did for Moses: "I will **protect** you because you acknowledge my name, and, if you call on me, **I will answer you, be with you in trouble,** then **honor** and **satisfy you**" (Psalm 91:14–16, paraphrased).

So the Lord has a simple template for us: We say His name, and He provides a tower of refuge and gives us protection and rest while in His care. In Moses's case, the Lord even took it upon Himself to declare His name on Moses's behalf. In effect, the Lord said, "Here's all my glory; here is my name offering you protection, confidence, refuge, and rest. Now go! Move! Will you do the assignment I have asked of you?"

Call on His Name

Have you ever felt so exhausted, sad, helpless, or confused that you don't know what to do with yourself? You desperately want to get out of your headspace—to escape. Maybe you're thinking really terrible thoughts that you can only utter to a spouse or a best friend as a release or a confession because you don't know where else to turn. Or maybe you're not able to process your feelings with anyone; you don't even know where to start. You're holding it all in, trying to bury it and move on. "It'll be fine," you tell yourself, but you're drowning. Things are weighing on you so hard that you're stuck in a state of worry and anxiety; deep down you think you're no good to anyone.

Per God's template, call on His name. Run to Him and allow Him to take it from there. Refuge and rest will be yours. Capture the negative, low-frequency thoughts by saying His name regularly, and you will begin to think new thoughts. You will start to realize that you are not battling these things alone, nor are you sitting in your suffering, confusion, sadness, or angst without tools. Your heart will begin to open and allow space for the Holy Spirit to enter. Your deepest desire, which is to be in union with God, will be met. You will feel something true, something real. And you'll begin to know what the lightness of walking in His presence means. You'll begin to experience all this by merely saying His name.

When we call out the Lord's perfect and precious name, it's a one-word powerful prayer.

Jesus goes even further to feed us more words to pray to Him. Clever Jesus. He knows how we operate and that most of the time, we just don't have the words. We don't know what to say.

Through the Lord's prayer though, He reminds us to not only call on His name but to pray that His will and intent are done here on earth and in the spiritual realm. He waits for us to say yes to our unique assignments that will carry out the good of His will. He waits for us to call out to Him: "Our Father, you are in Heaven; Holy is your name. Your Kingdom come; your will be done on earth as it is in heaven . . ." (Matthew 6:9–10, paraphrased).

The Futures We Create

God is not just a noun; *God* is also a verb. God moves, stirs, burns, shakes, quakes, walks, and whispers, doing whatever we need to experience Him. Through us, He shapes futures and creates paths. Time carries us forward and away from our past, but as His people, we have the power to choose what those paths look like. There's no shortage of intersecting roads; they are high or low, rocky or smooth, watery or muddy or bumpy. Some are isolated; others are crowded with strangers or friends. Some offer breathtaking views, while others are so oppressive that we can't escape quickly enough. Yet, in all of life, God moves in and around us constantly, just as we move through this world generation after generation.

As we noted previously, this world was created with invisible energy that produces very visible reactions. The Spirit, too, moves invisibly, but His presence becomes clear to those faithful to Him. The more we get to know God, the more we recognize His actions, His style, and His consistent character. We begin to rely on His unchanging promises, trusting that His will is steadfast and His love unfailing.

We are God's favorite thing. He invites us into His Kingdom now, not as a far-off destination, but as a reality we can experience today. His desire is that through intimately knowing His good and beautiful ways, we will understand ourselves and our imperfect nature so that we no longer want the two to be disconnected. He wants us to understand that He has remedied that disconnection through His son Jesus's death by crucifixion and resurrection and that eternal life and union with Him are available to each of us now. He longs to join us to Him and carry our burdens, sufferings, and even the mundane struggles of daily life. But the question remains: Will we accept His invitation? Do we want to be joined to Him?

He invites us to live here on earth with His boundless treasures filling our hearts. Through our choices and actions, we can create futures that see and know His boundless, unconditional, mega love for us. That kind of love leaves me astonished and amazed. It brings me to my knees in humility and gratitude. And from that place, like Moses, God calls us to rise and step into the assignments He has prepared for us.

When we return to Him, He meets us with reassurance: "I got you, so you got this." Whatever your "this" is in that moment, He promises to equip you. On the other side of fear and uncertainty lie His faithfulness and the fulfillment of His promises—all ready and waiting for us when we simply call on His name.

Recap

We've completed the first section of this book aimed at calling attention to two things in order to deepen our understanding of what it means to love the Lord our God with all our hearts. First, we considered the importance of keeping the physical heart of our cardiovascular system healthy by being good stewards of our temple bodies. Second, we explored ways to care for our figurative hearts, defined as our will or spirit. We can know God's will in our own lives by paying attention to His heart and intentions. When we align our heart with His, buckle up for an adventurous, fulfilling life.

God values our bodies and all its parts. After all, they are what Dallas Willard calls our "power pack," which God has assigned to us as the field of our freedom, growth, and development. There are boundless ways to care for your body through a positive mindset, taking in healthy foods, exercising, and resting. Walking the walk takes good stewardship over your temple body. You're three weeks into this program, which means you're doing it. You got this!

In the next section of this book, we will focus on the mind—how to love the Lord our God with all our mind. But first, let's get to this week's activities.

Activities Week 3

Heart (physical exercise): Upon waking, do the child's pose with gratitude. Then, set the timer on your phone for thirty seconds and run in place (or march with high knees if you prefer low impact) punching your arms in front of you.

Mind (cleanse): Do the rag doll/forward fold stretch. Get there by standing tall. Then soften or bend your knees deeply, and slowly melt your head and arms to the floor. Grab hold of your elbows, and release your lower back and the backs of your legs, keeping your knees soft. Let the contents of your mind spill off you. Breathe.

Soul (renew and restore): Each morning this week, write a full page or more in a stream of consciousness, also known as a brain dump. Don't think about what's going onto the page or judge it. Simply let it flow out of you.

Loving Others (scripture and prayer): Read Ephesians 2:10, which says, "*For we are God's masterpiece. He has created us anew in Christ Jesus, so we can do the good things He planned for us long ago.*" But declare it by stating it in the first person: "I am God's masterpiece. He has created me anew in Christ Jesus, so I can do the good things He planned for me long ago." Pray thanks; ask for help and guidance; and pray for God's power to enter your circumstance.

SECTION 2:

"Love the Lord Your God with All Your Mind"

CHAPTER 4:
INNER THOUGHTS AND CONSCIOUSNESS

Every thought we think is creating our future.

—Louise Hay

In the classic novel *The Picture of Dorian Gray*, Oscar Wilde tells the story of a man named Dorian who is admired for his extraordinary beauty.[14] Dorian becomes influenced by a pleasure-seeking man named Lord Henry whom he meets while having his portrait done by the artist Basil. Lord Henry convinces him that pursuing beauty is the most important thing in life. As a result, Dorian wishes that his portrait would age instead of himself. And that magically begins to happen. He goes on to live a life of indulgence and debauchery without the consequences affecting his appearance.

Dorian becomes involved with a beautiful actress named Sibyl. One night he invites his friends, Basil and Lord Henry, to see her perform. She gets nervous because Dorian is there, and her performance is less than stellar. Dorian's friends are unimpressed and mock him for only courting her for her beauty. Out of embarrassment he cruelly ends their relationship. Tragic events ensue, including Sibyl's suicide and Dorian's further descent into a life of depravity. With each sin, Dorian remains young and more beautiful while his portrait takes the brunt of it.

When confronted by the artist Basil about his lifestyle, Dorian reacts violently and decides to kill him. But it doesn't end there. A moment of conviction comes upon Dorian, and in desperation to absolve himself, he thinks that stabbing the portrait will do the trick. Thud!

His servants rush into the locked room only to find a disfigured, shriveled corpse curled up on the floor with a knife by its side. But there sits the portrait with its beauty restored.

Dorian's story is our story. It's a great representation of the consequences of living selfishly. He indulged in temptation and suffered the consequences of his immoral actions. It's also a story of hope lost. The reader's hope arrives when truth-telling friend Basil calls him out. Dorian is faced with a choice to turn from his evil ways, which began with his thoughts. And his thoughts housed his choices.

Active Consciousness

Our inner thoughts and what we choose to direct our attention to, which I'll call "active consciousness," have everything to do with how we develop as the main character in our own story.

Consciousness is one of those ambiguous terms that people hear, both in scientific and spiritual contexts, yet have difficulty describing. Consciousness is immaterial, so we can't touch it. Yet it can feel palpable at times. It can be felt within our inner being as an epiphany, for example. We can sense consciousness outside ourselves, like the discovery of new information that blows our minds.

Sometimes, consciousness can be passive like when someone is on life support in the ICU; we describe them as being "conscious" or "unconscious." Sometimes, we refer to our dreams as revealing something trapped in our "subconscious" mind. Or we ask someone who commits a malevolent action whether they were "conscious" of the harm they caused.

One dictionary definition describes *consciousness* as a person's awareness of understanding and realizing something.[15] In this way, consciousness is not merely passive but is active in some sense. I'm convinced that we can be participants in developing a desired state of consciousness by actively drawing our attention to something. And thankfully our great Creator has designed us biologically speaking to do such a thing.

Neuroscience is a relatively recent area of scientific and psychological focus. It deals with the structure, function, and development of the nervous system and brain. Science had to catch up with human instinct; neuroscience ties our physical body to our inner, intuitive being. When an individual is aware of that connection and discovers how to wield it in her own life, a door that once was closed swings wide open because what we think about directly relates to how we feel.

Active consciousness, or focused awareness, can be shaped and sharpened. Motivational speakers such as Toni Robbins, Mel Robbins, Ed Mylett, and Zig Ziglar have built their entire careers around helping people do just this. They have taught many people how to eliminate the mental and emotional blocks and barriers they set for themselves so they can reach their highest potential both personally and professionally.

Renewing Our Mind

In 1937, Napoleon Hill wrote one of the most popular business books of his day titled *Think and Grow Rich*. In this volume, Hill explained how by the power of thought, belief, and a fierce determination for a specific purpose, one can achieve extraordinary success and wealth.[16] He taught extensively about the importance of a positive attitude and taking action to achieve goals, similar to what some would later refer to as having a "growth mindset." This term has filtered its way through schools used to help students re-frame how they perceive certain experiences. Failure is not seen as a limit of the student's abilities, for example, but an opportunity to grow. And studies in epigenetics have taught us that we are not even bound to the DNA sequence we are born with. We can alter how our body reads a DNA sequence depending on our own behaviors and environment.

In *Breathe: A Life in Flow*, Brazilian mixed martial artist (MMA) Rickson Gracie and Peter Maguire capture the connection between the physical body and our inner, intuitive being in this way. Gracie says, "Curiosity coupled with courage allows you to go beyond your limits, venture into the unknown, and establish new limits that you never thought were possible. My curiosity always overpowered my fear."[17] He trained his mind and his body to become one of the most internationally sought after fighters and leaders in the MMA world. His training methods disrupted old thought patterns and stressed his body in a positive way so that he could become the best fighter in the world.

Gracie's entire lifestyle, from what he ate and drank to how and where he spent his time and with whom, prepared him to become the best MMA fighter in the world. He focused his awareness on those things that would support his goal.

Let's take a closer look at how we can face our limitations and fears with curiosity and courage as Gracie did. We can prepare our mind's renewal by understanding the unique design of our physical body and leveraging the machine that it is. Along these lines, the Apostle Paul gave this instruction: *"Do not conform to the pattern of this world but be transformed by the renewing of your mind. Then you will be able to test and approve what God's will is—His good, pleasing and perfect will"* (Romans 12:2 NIV).

We'll focus first on stimulating the command center of our body: our brain. We'll follow that by examining the spine—the area of our physical body responsible for helping us break through limits we've set for ourselves. It helps us tap into the mind, where consciousness is housed.

The spine is home to our central nervous system. And you may have heard it said, you're only as young as your spine is healthy. A closer look at four features associated with the spine can inform us of our need for unique and specific training to help nurture our mental, emotional, and physical health.

Sympathetic and Parasympathetic Nervous Systems

The sympathetic and parasympathetic nervous systems are an incredible part of our biological makeup. The two go hand in hand and are seen as stimulating inverse responses in the body. One is stress; the other is calm.

When the body is in a condition of stress, it's in a sympathetic state, or "fight or flight" as it's known. The sympathetic nervous system can be essential to survival; for example, early humans needed to take action when being chased by a lion or facing some other life-threatening situation. Hence, they had a fight-or-flight reaction. The *Encyclopedia Britannica* explains it this way:

> The sympathetic nervous system's response is characterized by the release of large quantities of epinephrine from the adrenal gland, an increase in heart rate, and increase in cardiac output, skeletal muscle, gastrointestinal vasoconstriction, and bronchial dilation. The overall effect is to prepare the individual for imminent danger. Chronic stress results in long-term stimulation of the fight or flight response which leads to constant production and secretion of epinephrine and hormones such as cortisol. Long-term stress induced secretion of these substances is associated with a variety of physiological consequence including high blood glucose levels, which can lead to type 2 diabetes and hypertension which can lead to cardiovascular disease.[18]

This tells us that the lasting effects from long-term fight-or-flight responses cross over to most of our body's health systems and can lead to poor breathing and also anxiety.

The Tummy (Solar Plexus)

Also part of this fight-or-flight system is the solar plexus, which is a complex system of radiating nerves found in the pit of the stomach. It plays an important role in the function of the stomach, kidneys, liver, and adrenal glands. And anxiety is a common cause of solar plexus pain.

I had a friend who had two kids and was going through a divorce, but I didn't know it at the time. Her younger daughter would come over to our house and relay the message from her mom that she needed to stay with us for the day because her mom had a "black hole in her tummy." It's a vivid and accurate image for anyone who has experienced something super stressful. She continued to show up at our house every so often over the following months due to the black hole in her mom's tummy.

Divorce—two becoming one and then breaking off into two again—is a painful process. Circumstances in life that wreck your heart and mind often burrow themselves into your physical body. They settle into specific areas and can take on a life of their own—even black holes in tummies. Here's the good news: In addition to equipping us with the fight-or-flight response, God designed us with a built-in calming system.

Negative stresses, whether from physical, emotional or spiritual factors, can cross over into the calm system, called the parasympathetic nervous system. The prefix "para" means alongside or beyond. This system is known as the "rest and digest" state. Picture a skydiver jumping out of a plane as the "active" sympathetic nervous system and the skydiver's parachute as the parasympathetic system, which is "passive," necessary and lifesaving.

The Vagus Nerve

The main nerve in the parasympathetic system brings us to the third feature associated with the spine, which is called the vagus nerve. It is the superhighway between your brain and your gut. And this nerve is highly impacted by stress. The wonderful news, however, is that when you're feeling high levels of stress, stimulating your vagus nerve can decrease your fight-or-flight response and calm your inflammatory stress hormones. According to Dr. Ashley Turner, author, licensed psychotherapist and leading Yoga-Meditation teacher, the benefits of stimulating the vagus nerve include: regulating food glucose, reducing inflammation levels, improving digestion, boosting immune function, supporting detoxification, improving metabolic function, calming stress, and fostering better mental health and neurotransmitter function.[19] A weak vagal tone can lead to opposite outcomes.

So far, to understand how the efforts of our physical body can help prepare the renewing of our mind, we've looked at some intricacies associated with the spine, which houses the sympathetic and parasympathetic nervous system, influences our solar plexus, and impacts the vagus nerve. Let's look next at the fourth feature associated with our parasympathetic nervous system.

The Diaphragm

Enter the powerful muscle of the diaphragm, which sits on the border of the ribs all the way around body and looks like no other muscle. Its shape looks somewhat like a parachute. And it indeed has a connection to the parasympathetic nervous system by being one of the most powerful indirect influences on it. Also, the vagus nerve runs right through the diaphragm. When we inhale, the diaphragm contracts, lifts, and flattens, and when we exhale the diaphragm relaxes and returns to its parachute-like shape. To stimulate the parasympathetic nervous system, we need to practice diaphragm breathing (aka balloon breath).

Taking Action to Bring It Together

So let's do it. Find a quiet place and sit up tall in a chair with your feet on the ground or the floor with your legs crossed. Turn your palms up, resting your hands on your knees or thighs. Relax your shoulders as far away from your ears as you can. Relax your jawbone. Read through the following breath practice first; then close your eyes and try this breathing technique.

- Breathe in through your nose, slowly, 1 – 2 – 3 – 4. Observe and feel your belly expand and inflate like a balloon.
- Breathe out through your mouth, lips slightly pursed, slowly 1 – 2 – 3 – 4. Feel your belly fall in toward your spine and hollow out. Slightly pause at the end of your exhale before inhaling again.

Now that you got it, set your timer on your phone for one minute and practice this breathing technique. If you need longer, extend to two or even three minutes. Then go back to your normal breathing pattern. Take a few moments to scan through your body—crown of the head to fingertips to toes—and feel the effects.

God's Prescription When You Feel Overwhelmed

Throughout Scripture, the concept of Jesus as "The Great Physician" is drawn from His role as the ultimate healer (e.g., Matthew 4:23, Mark 1:32–34, Luke 5:31–32, Isaiah 53:5, Matthew 9:12–13). He's the Doctor of all doctors. And since God is not only in the business of healing but also authoring life, He gives us a prescription for when we hit our breaking point. It's clearly outlined for us in Elijah's story.

Elijah is a prophet during a chaotic time in Israel (1 Kings 17–19). One day he finds himself running all day to escape being killed. He is scared. He is exhausted. During the hot pursuit, he becomes so discouraged and so tired that when he sees a tree, he sits down under it and gives up. I picture him sweaty, dirty, smelly, stumbling with maybe a bum knee, and panting from exhaustion. He's got nothing left in him, body and soul. He's having his mercy moment: "Dear God, make it stop!" We've all been there. Elijah prays that he might die. Then he goes to sleep.

When my kids were little and having a meltdown at bedtime, I'd hold them and say, "Go to sleep; it'll be a new day tomorrow." Similarly, Elijah had an angel visit him to comfort him, waking him up twice while he slept, telling him to get up, eat, and drink. The angel also acknowledged that the journey was too much for him. The angel didn't use the "keep your chin up" tactic; instead he validated Elijah's feelings and commiserated with him. The right words can be a healing balm. Other times sitting with people in their pain and suffering is all that's needed. No words.

Finally, when Elijah gets up, he's strengthened, and he had a major turnaround of attitude: Elijah went on from that place to travel forty days and forty nights. We'll come back to what happened next for Elijah but first a quick story about one of my finance clients named Sue.

In her mid-seventies, Sue opened up to me about her experience following the death of her husband twelve years prior. They had been married forty years when he died. She said:

> I was never actively suicidal, but I was passively suicidal, saying things to myself like, "Lord, if you took me in my sleep tonight, I wouldn't mind." But then I'd open my eyes the next morning and realize I was still there and think, "Well, there must be a reason." So I'd go on with life for one minute. And then, the next minute. Pretty soon I was up to doing something for fifteen minutes. Then I realized I could go longer. You never really get over it, but you learn how to live with it. My faith is what got me through it.

Sometimes, it's not about *your* why but having faith in God's why. After Elijah got his supernatural boost to get up and move, we learn why his prayer request to die was not granted: God is not done using him to fulfill His plans yet.

But it didn't take long for Elijah to fall back into his spell of despondency and run into a cave. Our time in the cave can feel like a tonic. We want to hide from the world, get away from the pressures, disappointments, betrayals, demands, and expectations. But God is always pursuing us, even in our cave.

Elijah is sad and frustrated at the current state of his nation:

> *And the word of the* LORD *came to him: "What are you doing here, Elijah?" He replied, "I have been very zealous for the* LORD *God Almighty. The Israelites have rejected your covenant, torn down your altars, and put your prophets to death. . . . I am the only one left, and now they are trying to kill me too."*
> —1 Kings 19:9–10 NIV

And guess what God does next? It's something familiar. *"The Lord said, 'Go out and stand on the mountain in the presence of the Lord, for the Lord is about to pass'"* (1 Kings 19:11 NIV). God gives Elijah the same glorious treatment Moses got.

Then, a wind comes and tears the mountain apart and shatters the rocks, but we learn that the Lord is not in the wind. Then comes an earthquake followed by a fire, but God isn't in those phenomena either. Then, finally, a gentle whisper comes, and Elijah pulls his cloak over his face and knows he's in the presence of the Lord. He goes and stands at the mouth of the cave (1Kings 19:11–13).

I picture Elijah scared, sinking into himself in the dark cave. Then with that whisper, everything changes. He's given supernatural strength and an overwhelming sense of readiness to step into the light of God. And in that state, the Lord gives him clear guidance. Elijah is to go back where he came from and anoint three new leaders that the Lord has selected; one of them, Elisha, will be Elijah's successor (1 Kings 19:15–16).

God didn't allow Elijah to die in his sleep, but he gave him an "out" so he could retire. In fact, Elijah never died. He just got whisked away to heaven on a horse-driven chariot when God was ready to give him the ultimate rest.

Recap of God's 8-Step Prescription

Elijah's story provides us the eight steps prescribed by Dr. God for when we hit our breaking point. Let's look at them one more time:

1. **Talk to God** about your problem (aka have your meltdown, knowing God is with you).
2. **Rest and sleep.**
3. **Lean on an angel of a friend or family member** who can care for you. Allow them to take something off your plate. Maybe they tidy up your house, watch your kids, make a meal or two, fold your laundry, or take over your project at the office. Share with them what's going on so they can have a chance to acknowledge the pain of what you're experiencing. Let them be with you in the cave.
4. **Hydrate and eat something healthy.**
5. **Stay in it**—whether you're high on energy or feeling despondent, pray for faithful confidence in God's purpose for you. The struggle is good.
6. **Spend some alone time with God** so you can hear His whisper in your heart.
7. **Listen** to His clear guidance—His call just for you.
8. **Go!**

Pay Attention to Your Thoughts

I recently heard Rudy Ruettiger as keynote speaker at a business luncheon. If you don't know Rudy Ruettiger's story, watch the 1993 film *Rudy*.[20] Rudy had spirit and heart but not the size or grades to play football for Notre Dame, which was his dream. With hard work he got into the school, played on the football team, and tackled the Georgia Tech quarterback in a final play. There isn't a person in the world who doesn't love the end of the movie where Rudy, the underdog turned hero, is carried off the field on his teammates' shoulders while the crowd is cheering, "Ru-dy! Ru-dy!"

During his speech, Rudy told us a story about getting a call inviting him to come to the White House when he was forty-five years old. He heard the White House Social Director's voice on the other end of the phone and paused in disbelief. He said in that moment, he knew he couldn't say his *goofy* thoughts out loud, as he called them. He realized that was a moment he had to "think like a CEO and fake it 'til he makes it." He didn't get called to the White House for knowing things, like who the fifth US President was. He got the call because of his heart, spirit, character, and courage. He quoted a common saying often attributed to Teddy Roosevelt: "People don't care how much you know until they know how much you care." Rudy pushed fear aside and believed that when you did, wild things could happen. He said, "God and his army of angels would make it so. A good attitude attracts good stuff."[21]

We can be our own worst enemy. Our negative minds and the lies we tell ourselves, whether crafted on our own or thrown on us by others, can take us down the path of living small. Our light begins to dim, and before we know it, we're hiding in the dark.

Our inner thoughts matter. Pay attention to what those thoughts are. They are directly related to how you feel. Active consciousness is asking God to take captive those "goofy" or negative thoughts. Remember Paul's advice: *"Do not be conformed to the pattern of this world, but be transformed by the renewing of your mind"* (Romans 12:2 NIV).

A life of trusting Jesus is a life of trusting that you can be fierce, brave, and courageous. It's a gift offered to us all, but not all of us choose to open it. If fear and timidity are holding you back from receiving that gift, you're not alone. Welcome to the club. That's where prayer comes in. Ask. Ask for a spirit of character, courage, and strength. Ask God to reveal your fears to you and be with you as you confront them. Living in God's kingdom is not a life of timidity or a life of comfort. It's a life filled with risk and purpose and adventure. And it has a life-giving impact on others.

Active consciousness, or focused awareness, can be shaped and sharpened. By focusing your awareness on how God sees you, you can change everything. If you spend time reading about who you are from His perspective, then believe what he's saying about you. This is not a comprehensive list, but here are a few things you will find in His word: You are His child, His beloved, His friend, a branch on His vine (in other words one with Him), chosen by Him, called by Him to live out your potential, blameless and pure through Him. This is your God-defined identity. And through His power and His faith in you, He will provide an abundance of bandwidth for you to go and keep moving. Whether it's getting up five minutes earlier each day to nurture your Temple body through diaphragm breathing, reaching goals to be your best at a craft, confronting a life of debauchery that's keeping you in darkness, staying in a never-ending situation minute by minute, or listening for a God-given out. You never know; he may have a horse-driven chariot waiting just for you.

Before we go to the next chapter where we discover how the power of prayer can renew our mind, let's dive into this week's exercises.

Activities Week 4

Heart (physical exercise): Upon waking, do the child's pose with gratitude. Then, move your spine in a cat/cow stretch, side to side, and twist (or rotate). These are three simple exercises you can use to move your spine all the ways it needs to go to stay lubricated: flexion/extension, laterally, and rotating.

- *Cat/cow:* On your hands and knees (knees below your hips, hands below your shoulders), inhale and draw your pelvis to the sky, taking your spine along with it as it arches up gently through to the neck. Then, exhale as your pelvis tucks in as if drawing toward your naval; the spine follows and rounds like a rainbow, and you tuck your chin into your chest. Repeat eight to ten times.
- *Lateral stretch (side to side):* Sit cross-legged (on a bolster or pillow if knees are tender) or on a chair. Inhale and raise your arms near your ears. Exhale; reach your left hand up and over, stretching your left side long

and gently place your right hand onto the floor (not crunching your right side, but lifting your bottom ribs away from your right hip). Breathe a few long, deep breaths before changing sides.
- *Rotation (twist):* Lie on your back and draw your knees into your chest. Then, gently drop your legs over to the left side, opening your arms out wide to the side (in one with your shoulders) and look over to your right arm. Breathe a few long, deep breaths before changing sides.

Mind (cleanse): Practice balloon breath each morning this week. Set your timer from one to three minutes and practice the diaphragm breathing technique that I call balloon breath. Breathe in through the nose, out through the mouth for a count of four each time. Focus on your belly expanding and then deflating.

Soul (restore and renew): Reflect and write about at least one area where you feel God is using you for a bigger purpose. Then, jot down where you'd like to be useful in the next five years. Is it related to your career; your physical health; or the spiritual, financial, relational, or educational aspects of your life? Carve out a few minutes each morning this week to explore and reflect on your thoughts. If you're married, share your discoveries with your spouse.

Love Others (scripture and prayer): Read Romans 12:1–2 each day this week. Before reading each day say this prayer: "Lord, please reveal to me what you'd like me to see and know today."

CHAPTER 5:
PRAYER AND GOD'S TIMING

Prayer is as necessary as the air, as the blood in our bodies, as anything to keep us alive—to keep us alive in the grace of God.

—Mother Teresa

In the comedy movie *Talladega Nights* starring Will Farrell and John C. Reilly who play race car driving best friends, Will Farrell begins the prayer around his family's dinner table with "Dear baby Jesus." He thanks baby Jesus for the KFC, Domino's pizza, and Taco Bell they're about to eat, for his two sons Walker and Texas Ranger, and for his hot wife. He asks Him to use His baby Jesus powers to fix his father-in-law's leg. His annoyed wife interrupts the prayer to remind him that baby Jesus grew up. Then they argue about which version of Jesus they each picture in their minds. His son pictures Jesus as a ninja fighting off an evil Samurai. Will Farrell doubles down. He resumes the prayer "Dear 8-pound 6-ounce newborn infant Jesus . . ."[22]

All jokes aside, I have a question for you. If there is one thing you would like to ask God for in your life, what would it be? I asked myself that question while out on a walk one day. The answer was so clear and within reach of my heart. I want my two children, Rook and Pepper, to seek God hungrily in their hearts through all the stages of their lives. I envision them going through their teens and young adult years, then getting married and raising kids. I envision them living their lives in a constant odyssey, saying yes to opportunities where they can shine for God and for others. Their lives would be filled with struggles, adventure, whimsy, and wonder all while, deepening their character. I pray that they will let me be a part of that with them.

I asked my husband the same question. His answer was much broader: peace on earth, good will toward men. I'm glad we are a team. When I shared my response with him, he philosophized that my prayer seemed pretty selfish and followed that by asking me if I want to take away our kids' free will. Oh boy. An interesting conversation followed, but I'm glad Jesus doesn't judge our prayers. He simply wants to have some time with us—talking, not talking, saying the wrong things, saying the right things; it doesn't matter. He just wants to be with us.

The fact that we have a channel by way of prayer to someone as mega as God is incredible when you really think about it. Our all-knowing, all-powerful, present-everywhere God has created that connection with little 'ole us. And it says something about how God sees us that we have that kind of lifeline. We are important to Him; the things on our minds and hearts are important to Him. And He wants to hear everything from us.

Take your kids for example. Do you want to hear what they're thinking—what they're struggling with and trying to sort out? Do you want them to come to you with questions? Or when they need comfort? How about when they make a mistake and exhibit genuine remorse instead of lying, denying, or blaming? This is the same type of heart-to-heart connection God our Father desires with us.

How about your spouse? When we spend time talking with our spouse without distraction, we have the chance to search each other's hearts and learn more about one another—what we want, and what's important to us. Making time for this deeper kind of connection consistently makes for fresh, interesting, and life-changing conversations whether you've been married two months or twenty years. In the same way, God covets time alone with us when we become calm and quiet, making space for Him. We invite Him to enter our heart and in turn, He reaches our soul.

Oftentimes, we don't even have the words to communicate with God. Remember the one-word prayer? In Romans we learn:

> *The Spirit helps us in our weakness. We do not know what we ought to pray for, but the Spirit himself intercedes for us through wordless groans. And He who searches our hearts knows the mind of the Spirit, because the Spirit intercedes for God's people in accordance with the will of God.*
> —Romans 8:26–27 NIV

God wants us to connect so badly with Him through prayer that He even provides us the ideas, thoughts, and words. He can shift us away from our woeful loneliness. There is no right way or right time to pray. Let's look at two stories where the power of prayer changed the future.

Hezekiah, an Old Testament King of Judah, prayed a prayer that appeared to cause God to change His mind (2 Kings 20:1–6; Isaiah 38:1–5). This is how the situation unfolded: Hezekiah becomes very ill, and Isaiah the prophet visits him and tells him to get his house in order because he is going to die. But Hezekiah feels he has work to do to lead the fight against their enemy, the Assyrians. He's not ready to die. When Hezekiah hears the message from God through Isaiah, he turns his face to the wall, prays to the Lord reminding Him of how faithful and devoted he's been to Him, and weeps bitterly.

Have you ever prayed in that way just crying out to God? If so, it was probably a very serious situation. For Hezekiah it was literally life or death. At moments such as this, it feels easy to lean on God. It becomes crystal clear that we need Him and that we are not in control; we're at our breaking point.

When Hezekiah turns to the wall, he tunes into God. And he prayed out loud. Oftentimes, prayer is private thoughts in private moments when we tune out the external world, and the eyes of our heart look upward and inward. These are the moments we can call on God's name. When we do, He welcomes us into the frequency of His kingdom, power, and glory. And in that realm, there are endless possibilities.

Hezekiah's prayer may seem like a ridiculous attempt to bargain with God almost as if he is saying, "Hey, God, I've been a really good person . . . faithful to you, so . . . how about me not dying." But God still hears his cries, and as Isaiah is about to leave, he does an about-face, because he has a new message from God to deliver to Hezekiah. Isaiah tells Hezekiah that God has heard his prayer and seen his tears, and He is going to heal him. In three days, Hezekiah is to go to the temple of the Lord; God promises to add fifteen years to his life. And Isaiah has more good news: At God's pleasure and because of His promise to Hezekiah's forefather King David, He will deliver him and the city from the Assyrian king.

God went above and beyond in answering Hezekiah's prayer. He does that—giving beyond our own imaginations, even though we don't deserve it. C. S. Lewis said:

> It would seem that Our Lord finds our desires not too strong, but too weak. We are half-hearted creatures, falling about with drink and sex and ambition when infinite joy is offered us. . . . We are far too easily pleased.[23]

When we lean on God in all our moments, not just when we're broken down, we are in tune with the source of infinite joy. So go ahead . . . pray for the big and the bold, the impossible. The thoughts and desires in our hearts through prayer just might shift the channels of God's heart. They just might change His mind.

And God can shift the channels of other people's hearts too. Our second story features a woman named Esther.

Enter Babylon

Esther's story is told in chapters 1–4 of the book of Esther; it is summarized here. Esther is a lovely young woman, being raised by her older cousin Mordecai since her parents had died. They are Jewish and are among those exiled from Jerusalem by King Nebuchadnezzar of Babylon. At the time of Esther's story, the Persians are in power, and King Xerxes is on the hunt for a new queen. Esther is one of many women in 127 provinces under his edict to be brought to the palace for the ultimate beauty pageant.

She and the other young women begin twelve months of beauty treatments under the management of a eunuch named Hegai. During that time, Esther's cousin Mordecai frequently paces outside the palace checking on her. God's presence shows up in people. And God is with her through Mordecai's care and protection.

Mordecai hears the wonderful news that Esther pleases Hegai; she's won him over. So he moves her up in the line and gives her the secrets for how to win the king over, which she does. God shifts the channels of King Xerxes's heart toward her. The invisible hand of God is at work. And the king is attracted to her in every way, more than all the other women, so he makes her queen.

There is just one catch: They don't know each other that well, which means that the king doesn't know about her Jewish background and nationality. And at Mordecai's guidance, Esther intentionally withholds this information from him.

Fast-forward to the next scene where we find Mordecai once again pacing outside the palace checking in on his cousin who is now Queen Esther. He overhears two of the king's officers who guard the doorway conspiring to assassinate King Xerxes. So Mordecai relays the message to Esther who passes the intel along to King Xerxes. An investigation takes place, and he learns that news of the plot to kill him is legitimate. He has the guards hanged on the gallows, all credit, albeit with no fanfare, going to Mordecai.

But another force is at work.

Enter the dark and sinister Haman who gets elevated to the highest point of honor by King Xerxes. Everyone at the king's gate of the palace is standing to praise him, except Mordecai. As it turns out, Haman has a huge ego. Burning with anger, he is fixated on the one person not paying him honor. So Haman does some digging and finds out that Mordecai is a Jew, and he wants revenge. It is not enough that Mordecai should suffer for not praising him; Haman takes it a thousand times further. In effect, he tells King Xerxes, "Hey, if this is a problem for me, it could be a bigger problem for you. This guy's people are scattered throughout your kingdom. They have very different customs from us, and it is not in your interest to tolerate them." Xerxes adores Haman and the large sum of money he promises to pay into the king's treasury if the king issues another edict to have all the Jews throughout the kingdom killed.

The plot thickens.

The world is not without terrible people. In fact, if someone is terrible enough times, it gets easier and easier. Dorian Gray got so far into his cruelty that there was no going back. The scary thing is that we're all capable of this. We face decision points along the way, and most of us make the right choice before things go too far, even when it's hard. We know the peace that comes with handling mistakes well. A mature, self-aware person sacrifices their selfishness to do what's right. We do it for our kids, we do it for the sake of others, and we do it so we can sleep at night. We'll do what it takes to have harmony in our own mind and heart. And whether we acknowledge it or not, that's God moving in us—nudging us and stirring our hearts.

No one has ever said that practicing the way of God is easy, but within our hearts exists a teacher, pointing us in the right direction. And He has not left us without tools to follow His path.

For Such a Time as This

Haman's evil and unjust influence is at play (Esther 4:1–14). There was fasting, weeping, and wailing throughout every province when Jews read the edict; no one was more troubled than Mordecai. Esther hears about his distress, and he urges her to plead to the king for her people.

But Queen Esther is scared. Persian law demanded that anyone, even the queen, who enters into the king's presence without being summoned, must be killed, unless the king extends the royal scepter to them.

It's Mordecai's turn to be brave at all costs. He goes to Esther in wisdom and tells her that if she stays silent, she will not escape the order of the king either. He adds, *"Who knows if perhaps you were made queen for just such a time as this"* (Esther 4:14)? This is Esther's moment.

Now it's her turn to tune the external world out. The eyes of her heart look upward and inward, and she finds her courage. She trusts in God's power in this dire circumstance. Esther is emboldened and agrees to make a move. What a difference one conversation can make. She gets Mordecai to rally all the Jews to fast for three days along with her and her maids. She is resigned to perish if that's where her courage and their faithful efforts take her.

Sometimes, when we pray, we turn away from people and look only to God. Other times, we rally the troops. Sometimes, the collective heart and mind turn toward a single bold prayer for things to change course. In this case, the Jews pray for the influence of evil to be stopped and for a leader's decision to be upturned. We must pray and have faith that even if God's justice is not seen in this world, it will be seen in the next. Sometimes, it means being uncertain and scared, and praying anyway. It's recognizing that maybe you are in your position of influence for such a time as this. You must have faithful confidence in God's good and right plan for you, because He loves you.

Three days later (Esther 5), Esther gets dolled up and the king sees her standing at the inner court hoping to speak with him. Channels shift in the king's heart again. He is very happy to see her, and he extends the royal scepter and says he will give her whatever she asks.

She wants Haman and the king to attend a banquet she is throwing for them. King Xerxes is pleased and agrees. And later at that banquet, he lets her know he will give her whatever she asks. She wants to throw a second banquet—in honor of Haman and the king, she says. It's there she will tell the king what she really wants.

Haman is ecstatic to get these invitations from the queen. But as he leaves the palace, he sees Mordecai, not standing to praise and honor him. And Haman is very bothered, once again. He goes home and gloats to his wife and friends about how much money he has and his many children; he tells them that Queen Esther adores him enough to throw two banquets in his honor. But there's this one pesky problem—Mordecai. Consoling him, his wife and friends encourage him to build gallows just for Mordecai and eliminate the nuisance.

When I was growing up my dad would say, "Surround yourself with upbeat people." It was a quote he adopted after reading Lee Iacocca's biography.[24] Who you surround yourself with matters: *"Bad company corrupts good character"* (1 Corinthians 15:33). I wonder what circumstances were involved with the evolution of Haman's terribleness and why he attracted other terrible people into his inner circle. But no matter, God's plan for the good of His people continues to unfold in the book of Esther.

Later that night (Esther 6–7), King Xerxes can't sleep. He requests the book that chronicles his reign be read to him. Lo and behold, he hears the record of the thwarted assassination plot of the king's officials that Mordecai had uncovered. The king inquires of his attendants whether Mordecai had been honored and recognized for this act of service. He is surprised to learn that nothing had been done for him. The king decides that this oversight must be remedied as soon as possible. So he asks his attendants who of his inner circle is standing nearby, and sure enough, Haman is right outside waiting to speak to the king about hanging Mordecai on the gallows. Talk about wrong place, wrong time.

The king wants Haman brought in and asks him what he thinks he should do for a man that he wants to honor. Who else would puffed-up Haman think the king is referring to except himself? So he goes on about how this person of honor should be placed on a royal horse wearing a royal robe paraded in all the streets for people to hear that this is how the king treats those he honors. The king tells him to go do all of that—for Mordecai.

Here's where the story gets even better. Haman goes home to his wife and friends totally despondent. And they have changed their tune. They start advising him not to go against Mordecai because he is a Jew, and they have heard that God of the Jews is powerful. Just then, a palace eunuch comes to take Haman away to the second banquet Queen Esther has prepared for him.

There at the second banquet when the king asks what Esther's petition is, she finally tells him. She confesses and discloses the secret she has been keeping from him. Esther pleads, "Spare me my life and the life of my people. We have been sold for destruction and slaughter and annihilation" (Esther 7:3–4, paraphrased). The king is shocked and asks who would do such a thing.

She points at Haman. The king rages. He storms out to the palace garden for some fresh air. When he comes back inside, he finds Haman hanging on Queen Esther at her couch begging for his life. The king is even more enraged after taking in the scene and orders that Haman be hung on the gallows prepared for Mordecai. That's poetic justice.

God's Time – Our Time

With God, all things happen at the right place and right time for the good of those who love Him. And if you're not sure about the timing of things in your life, ask God to show you. He'll show up and reveal to you what once was a mystery. But God's time is often not our time. When we try to fit Him into our time frame and our own agenda, we often lose connection and trust in Him. I've only recently come to truly know this.

Overachieving Type A personalities are goal oriented. And it's easy to become reliant on characteristics associated with reaching those goals. Being ambitious, organized, focused, and great at multitasking helped me get where I was going when I wanted to go there. I would do whatever it took to reach a goal, but I had to learn a big lesson in failure to change my ways.

I took a yearlong course to get some new letters behind my name. I loved the course and passed all the exams; then it was time to study for the board exam. I kept telling myself: I must pass the board exam to get the letters . . . only three more months. But the enjoyment left me like a child losing the grip of their helium balloon. My husband pointed out the obvious: that I was giving up a lot of what would be precious memories with my family in pursuit of this goal. But I pressed on. In the end, I failed the exam. And I did not take it well. I fell apart. It took a few days of tears and encouragement from friends to realize that this failure was a gift. Something had to give.

Around that time, my friend Anna recommended that I read *The Seven Spiritual Laws of Yoga* by Deepak Chopra. I appreciated the book and its emphasis on incorporating breath work, meditation, and movement into our daily life. Reading different philosophies has always fascinated me.

A section in the book, titled "The Law of Detachment," hit me right where I needed it. It explained that "the essence of the Law of Detachment is to have your intentions clearly in your awareness while you maintain an attitude of *Thy will be done*."[25] Chopra further explains:

> Practicing detachment and embracing uncertainty, you relinquish your need to hold on to the past, which is the only thing that is known. Being open to what is happening rather than trying to control how things unfold, you experience the excitement, adventure, exhilaration, and mystery of life.[26]

Control—it's a real struggle and hit the bull's-eye. And I was convicted. If someone had asked me what I feared, I would have said, "Nothing." I didn't think I had any fears, besides big dogs off leash. But once the concept of my need to control outcomes had been identified, I realized the source of it was fear. What would my life look like if I didn't achieve? If I didn't meet the expectations that I thought others had of me? Would I lose my edge and get nowhere in life?

I reflected on this fear and began to practice ways of eliminating it. I came to understand when I'm able to surrender my desired timing of things, my strategic outcome, my agenda, and even my dreams to God, He shows up in bigger and better ways than I could ever imagine. And more than that, I carry God's peace in my heart along that journey rather than carrying worry, anxiety, and control. That was a watershed moment for me.

How did I get there? I laid the fear and need to control down at God's feet through prayer, journaling, and getting into His Word. I asked Him to adjust my ways and thoughts about it; then I trusted that He would. I thanked Him for sending wise words of guidance and encouragement through friends.

And here's the big one: I had faith. I had faith in His bigger and better ways for me to be great in the roles He called me to as wife, mom, and wealth advisor to my clients—without me defaulting to my Type A ways to do so.

Does that mean He doesn't want us to work hard to go after the dreams He places in our hearts? Absolutely not. We are called to move, not coast.

God invites us to live life in a way that we won't regret anything when we're in our eighties; He expects us to take chances, take risks, work smart, and work hard. And the first step to living this kind of fully committed life is to do the inner work of confronting things that matter.

A Blueprint for Inner Work

A few years back I had a conversation with a divorced middle-aged woman who told me she prayed hard for her financial situation to improve. She keeps faith that it will, she told me. My heart was warmed until she went on. She told me that she has a hard time not spending. "On what," I asked. Weekends in the San Francisco area to visit her son; they have a new grandbaby, so she buys gifts for him. Her son's wife doesn't like to have her stay with them, so she has to pay for a cheap hotel. When she's home, she mostly eats out during the week because she works and has no time to cook. She likes brand-name clothes, shoes, and jewelry. She confessed that she doesn't budget, and she feels bad because she doesn't give any part of what she earns to her church. She worries because she doesn't have enough saved. And with little invested for retirement, she fears she'll have to work forever. But she's believin' Jesus for it.

My friends, faith is meant to be active. Taking practical steps in the process of trusting God is essential. And we can pray for the people we come across who are in this situation—as frustrating as it is. When they have an unwillingness to change their behavior, prayer seems futile. Yet, one could say that this woman's willingness to spill her situation to me was an answer to prayers. After she shared, I could try to help her devise a plan to couple her faith with responsibility and action.

First, I guided her to begin a discovery process to reveal the root of her spending. We took it one by one, naming the fear around each issue. I heard her say, "I fear losing time with my son and grandson." That's fair. Then she said, "I fear not looking my best if I don't buy new things." Alternatives abound. "I don't want to change my eating style," she explained. There are other convenient, less expensive options. Sadly, she shared, "I fear how little my emergency and retirement savings are." We can run the numbers and see where she stands.

Fear and control are at the root of every one of these things. I encouraged her to write down each of those issues and then dive in with some action items. She thought through some solutions:

> I can see when my son and family can visit me, or we can meet halfway at a park for a picnic. I'm going to look for discount websites or local secondhand stores known for having high quality clothes and jewelry. I'll evaluate pre-made meals at the grocery stores around me. I'll look at my

monthly cash flow and commit to a dollar amount I'd like to give to my church. Finally, let's run those projections you mentioned to see if I'm on track to retire or generate a plan so I can.

That awareness helped her to be more specific with her prayers:

> Lord, give me motivation to improve my money situation. Help me to be honest with my son about my budget, so we can brainstorm new, less expensive experiences to be together. Shift the channels of my heart with my daughter-in-law to help us bond. Show me healthy and inexpensive meal solutions. Open my fist to be more financially generous. What I have comes from you only; show me how you'd like me to use it. Help me to be a good steward of my money.

Her original prayer, "I'm believin' Jesus for it," opened like an accordion fan. By confronting the root of her financial issues, her seemingly empty prayer became an answered prayer. Her faith empowered her toward goals with confidence that God was with her in the process.

To recap, the 5-step blueprint:

1. Be willing to confront the issue.
2. Discover what's at the root of your issue. Why is that issue important to you?
3. Name the fears around the issue. Write them down.

4. What action items can shift your perspective on the issue and the issues around it?
5. Be honest. Then become more specific with your prayers.

The Treasure in Our Hearts

In the Gospel of Matthew, Jesus teaches us that if we don't lay down what's most important to us, we will have a hard time following Him:

> *If any of you wants to be my follower, you must give up your own way, take up your cross, and follow me. If you try to hang onto your life, you will lose it. But if you give up your life for my sake, you will save it. And what do you benefit if you gain the whole world but lose your own soul?*
> —Matthew 16:24–26

Jesus knows how important our dreams and agendas are to us. But He also knows how we operate. Our priorities are so skewed. We easily put anything or anybody that gives us a sense of security, identity, and belonging first in our lives. And this starts to poke holes in our foundation. We end up building a house on sand and filling it with counterfeits. Experiences and things intended to bring us happiness and pleasure instead, sink us into emptiness, worry, unease, and a longing for something not within reach.

And it's so easy on this side of the grave for something or someone else to crowd God out of our minds and hearts. This is why God listed the greatest commandment first.

When something is listed first, that usually means it's the number one priority: *"You must not have any other god but me"* (Exodus 20:3).

We can't serve two "gods" at once—earthly things like money, power, success, fame, control, **and** the things of heaven. We either give God our projects and agendas, concerns and issues, temptations, and desires, or we take them on ourselves. Scripture teaches that one "god" is always reigning in our lives over the other. But when we prefer God over everything else and follow Him with all our heart, all our mind, all our soul, and all our strength, we have a sense of shalom, which is wholeness, completeness, and calm. And we're building our house on a strong foundation, not sand.

In this chapter we focused on prayer and God's timing in our lives. We learned that through prayer and listening to the voice of God in our hearts, we can build a solid foundation for our life. We also learned to turn our hearts upward and inward in prayer, as Hezekiah did. We learned to ask God for patience and trust as our lives unfold in His time, for motivation to turn away from our fears and attitudes of control, and for Him to bring us the people who will help protect us, like Mordecai protected Esther. We also ask Him to give us words of wisdom that give us the confidence to know we are in our place of position for such a time as this—a time to be courageous—a time to change the course of the world and put evil on the gallows—a time to live a life of risk and adventure—and a time to celebrate because of what God has done in you and through you.

We're coming up on the final chapter in section 2, "Love the Lord Your God with all Your Mind." In it, we'll explore the potential of our bodies and minds through three techniques: meditation, yoga, and breath work. But before we do, let's get to practicing this week's activities.

Activities Week 5

Heart (physical exercise): Upon waking, do the child's pose with gratitude. Then do twenty squats. Start with feet hip width distance apart. Sit your hips back as far as you can on the way down keeping your chest tall and your spine long. You can also do this from a chair: standing up, then sitting back down twenty times. Breathe—inhaling on the way down and exhaling on the way up.

Mind (cleanse): Stand tall and perform balloon breath. Pay attention to the breath pushing into every corner of your body: toes, fingertips, back, ribs, belly, and crown of your head.

Soul (restore and renew): Like the woman who was overspending and praying seemingly empty prayers, what issue is bothering you in your life? Are you willing to confront it? Go through these steps:

1. Name one issue.
2. What's at the root of that issue?
3. Name the fears, anxieties, worries, or desires around that issue. Write them down.
4. Dive in with specific action items.
5. Be more specific with your prayers about the issue.

Love Others (scripture and prayer): Pray for God to reveal His Spirit to you over the words in Philippians 4:6–7:

> *Don't worry about anything; instead, pray about everything. Tell God what you need, and thank him for all he has done. Then you will experience God's **peace, which exceeds anything we can understand. His peace will guard your hearts and minds as you live in Christ Jesus.*** (emphasis added)

CHAPTER 6:

REFLECTING THE CREATOR THROUGH MIND-BODY TECHNIQUES

Be still, and know that I am God!

—Psalm 46:10

Picture an ocean wave. Now feel into your body: head to fingertips to toes. The wave begins at your feet and as you inhale, the water comes up to the crown of your head. The wave pulls back into the ocean as you imagine it flowing back down to your feet. Everything the water touches feels warm and relaxed and begins to let go. Breathe in and the warm water travels up through your feet, legs, hips, belly, chest, arms, along the sides of your neck and up to the crown of your head. Breathe out and the water travels down your spine, shoulders, arms, legs, and over your toes.

If you wake up in the middle of the night and can't get back to sleep, this body scan meditation might do the trick. I've tucked my kids into bed with it a few times. And when my daughter was ten, she even led me into drowsiness with it in a role reversal.

At the core of cultivating a life of inner and outer alignment are practices like meditation, yoga, and breath work. They are an integral part of integrative medicine, which point us to a big distinction. Traditional Eastern medicine approaches an individual's symptoms in holistic terms. It addresses healing by the whole of the person, how we live and our experiences. Our focus in the West is on a dysfunctional aspect of physiology.

"Med," which is the root of words such as *medicine, remedy, mediator,* and *meditation,* generally connects to ideas of being in the middle, healing, or balance. "Med" also means "to take appropriate measures."[27] It implies action, moving from a particular state to an improved one. Let's take a closer look at how we can do that through three mind-body techniques: meditation, yoga, and breath work.

Meditation

It's difficult to put a single definition on the term *meditation* because it's so experiential. Depending on who you're talking to and what their background and experiences are, you'll get different descriptions. I've heard some say meditation means emptying your mind; others say it means awareness of what your mind thinks about. Some describe it as letting positive, repetitive words sink into your heart. And others believe that it's simply time for reflection while sitting in stillness and solitude.

Different nuances no doubt, but the idea is the same. I'm convinced that meditation has three fundamental insights.

First, meditation means that we step away from noise and enter into quiet and that we come away calmer and more centered. The negative and unnecessary feelings we carried into the quiet time are offloaded. Our minds feel clearer and sharper than before. We feel more prepared to take on whatever comes at us.

Second, meditation is biological. We are made in the image of God, and as previously mentioned, God has body parts: back, face, and hands; He also has a mind. God says, *"My thoughts are not your thoughts"* (Isaiah 55:8a NIV). His mind is perfect. Ours is not. We must exercise and strengthen our minds to honor and empower our temple body.

Earlier I referenced Dr. Curt Thompson's book *Anatomy of the Soul* from which, we learned that our brain's neuroplasticity is created by aerobic exercise, mental attentiveness, and novel learning experiences. Thompson says, "Neuroscience research confirms that mindful meditative exercises that stretch and challenge the internal mechanism of the brain enhance the integration of the pre-frontal cortex."[28] Simply put, our physical brain affects our mind and thoughts. And why is the pre-frontal cortex so important? It sits at the front of the brain and performs high-level, complex functions such as problem-solving, impulse control, decision-making, and personal expression such as perseverance and motivation.

The third insight is that biblical meditation can lead to spiritual transformation. But how do God's own words guide us to meditate? Meditation was common in Bible times. However, there is a fundamental difference between biblical meditation and meditation exercises meant purely for relaxation, such as the "body scan." In biblical meditation, the focus is not just on calming the mind but on centering one's thoughts on God—He is never far from the person's mind.

"I will reflect on all you have done and ponder your mighty deeds," the poet writes in Psalm 77:12 (BSB). Dr. Curt Thompson says taking a verse like this and allowing the images you see and the words you hear as you meditate on it can change your neural networks. Furthermore, he believes that if you do this every day for six weeks, you will be able to draw upon the images and positive emotions that come from that practice when a stress-inducing experience comes at you.[29]

Let's try another biblical meditation exercise. Consider God's Word in the following Scripture passage and replace what you're worrying about with what He wants you to think about?

> *Look at the ravens. They don't plant or harvest or store food in barns, for God feeds them. And you are far more valuable to him than any birds! Can all your worries add a single moment to your life? And if worry can't accomplish a little things like that, what's the use of worrying over bigger things."*
> —Luke 12:24–26

Let's pause and address something important. Many people try meditating, then throw in the towel when their "monkey mind" takes over. "It doesn't work for me," they say. "I can't meditate. My mind doesn't stop going. I can't sit still for that long." This is where setting aside a few minutes each day comes in. We have to start somewhere. In the same way we move our bodies every day, we also need to quiet our minds. We walk before we run. Meditation is no different. It takes a commitment to practice.

So let's try it. Retreat from the world. Set your timer for two minutes. Sit comfortably in a chair or on the floor with the *raven* verse from Luke in your hand. Read through it, twice. Then close your eyes and sit still. Allow the powerful imagery of this verse to flood your mind. By the Holy Spirit, these words have the power to supernaturally transform us. They renew our mind. They penetrate our soul. In this way, meditation becomes an act of worship.

Yoga

In the Christian culture, there are various perspectives with doing yoga. For some it's compatible; for others, it's conflicting. I've thought about this a lot over my twenty-plus years of practicing and teaching. And I have four thoughts about the topic.

First, yoga is an ancient technology, which benefits our mental, emotional, and physical well-being. With modern technology, people take drugs to combat many of the symptoms so many Americans are battling today. Although pills are needed in some instances, we have somehow become slaves to the acceptability of taking a pill to combat anxiety, depression, and many of the diseases associated with the Western lifestyle. Instead of being proactive, being open-minded, or giving some of the ancient methods a shot, we are conditioned to take physician-prescribed drugs.

Betty is a great example of choosing to leverage this ancient technique for her overall well-being. When I met Betty, she was eighty-five years old and had a physique that a woman of any age would admire. She practiced yoga with me once a week for fifteen years. She was a mother, grandmother, and missionary who faced a new role as widow. She dropped off for a couple months after her husband of fifty years died. Then quietly and sporadically, she kept showing up. About a year later, Betty was back. One day, she pulled me aside to describe the depths of her grief, and she hugged me. Attending yoga class was one of the things that helped pull her out of her grief, she told me.

Second, people with mature faith have asked me how I reconcile my faith and doing yoga. At first, I wasn't sure what I needed to contend with. Quite simply I'd think, it just makes me a better me. But the question has merit.

The Bible teaches that we are spiritual beings in a material world. Yoga has its roots in Hinduism; therefore, by practicing yoga, you could be opening gates to worship in a way God doesn't intend for you. He wants to be number one. Above all our faith is worth guarding, so why risk it?

And I'm nostalgic about yoga. I mentioned that I grew up as a competitive gymnast, dancer, then cheerleader. When I found yoga, it was an adapted form of those things that my body could tolerate as I got older. And I hope to continue doing it until the tomb. My daily home practice relaxes my mind and body, so when I do sit down to read the Bible, journal, and pray, I'm more focused. I have an openness about me where I can suck out everything I need as the Spirit reveals it to me.

This leads me to a question and my third point: Am I justifying doing yoga? That is, am I going my own way, holding onto a treasure I haven't yet surrendered to God. I've prayed the

REFLECTING THE CREATOR THROUGH MIND-BODY TECHNIQUES

prayer asking God to shift my thoughts and feelings about yoga if it's not serving me or others well. I listen for God's voice, and I keep hearing that it's beneficial for me. God is the resource for all and from all. And yoga is an activity that allows God to use me as a conduit for impacting my life and the lives of those around me in the greatest of ways. But is it beneficial for everybody?

This is where the primary conflict between yoga and Christianity stems. Here are a couple examples of when not to practice yoga.

My friend Julie, a former yoga instructor, who was raised in the church spent years involved with the occult, drugs, alcohol, and sexual promiscuity in Los Angeles. She heard Jesus's call to her later in life. She realized her mind went empty while teaching, and she felt susceptible to falling back into her old lifestyle. She knew in her heart the way to remain in Him was to walk away from teaching yoga and close that door behind her. God asked her to follow Him by leaving it. She obeyed and received His treasure and riches that sat above all else.

Also, it's important to note that a spirit of confusion can infiltrate the mind of a yoga practitioner. Yoga's roots are deeply intertwined with Hindu spirituality, which acknowledges multiple gods and goddesses, in contrast to the Christian belief in the singular and sovereign Lord of the Bible. My friends involved in deliverance work have shared compelling stories about how this can lead people astray. On a positive note, these accounts often culminate in significant breakthroughs in people's lives after they have severed ties with practices like yoga.

Whatever activity we find ourselves in, it is crucial to fiercely guard our hearts and minds. Our actions need to be in line with the truth of our faith. If any activity leads you away from Jesus or instructs you to empty your mind, cease immediately—it is not the right path. Persisting in this will lead to despair. And that's not God's heart for us.

On the other hand, if something draws you closer to Jesus, makes you feel better **in** your person and **as** a person, enables you to operate at your optimal level for all the roles you've been called to, and allows you to display who Jesus is and serve others better, then you're going the right way.

Jesus wants to be known and found, and He will guide us toward or away from something in an effort for us to see Him or hear Him. And that's what counts: being obedient when we hear God's voice. When we're willing to listen to Him, He kindly speaks to us. And when dealing with issues that have gray areas of application across different cultures, we have to be careful not to "hear for others."

If you are interested in practicing meditation, yoga, and breath work and you've prayed to invite God into that desire, then let Him guide you there—or not. But don't let what others have told you about it, fears, or a predisposed bias close you off from the potential it may have in your life. So have a conversation with God, and let Him take you where He wants you to go.

If you're considering taking a yoga class at home, in the gym, or at a studio, I recommend being mindful of two things: first, choosing a style of yoga that meets you where you are and second, finding an instructor whose approach resonates with you. Many studios offer introductory sessions, providing a chance to ask meaningful questions and get a feel for each instructor's unique style. This experience can help you decide whether a particular studio is the right fit. If you feel comfortable and excited to join a class, go! For those interested in practicing at home, the Yogaglo app is an excellent resource to explore various instructors, styles, and classes to find what works best for you.

Breath Work

The mysteries of the mind continue to unfold, and breath work is gaining recognition in the medical community for its profound benefits. According to WebMD, physical advantages of breath work include balanced blood pressure, more time in deep sleep, reduced symptoms of PTSD and trauma, stronger respiratory function, improved immune health, and stress hormone release. Emotional benefits include fewer feelings of depression and anxiety, improved mental focus, reduced addictive behaviors, emotional healing, and an increased sense of contentment and joy. These effects stem from breath work's ability to alkalize blood pH, provide anti-inflammatory benefits, and positively impact the central nervous system.[30]

Research also explores the connection between breath and brain function. For example, a 2022 Smithsonian article explains that, since the 1980s, neuroscientists have studied a brainstem network that sets respiratory rhythm. This discovery has led to further research showing that breathing influences broad areas of the brain, particularly those affecting emotions and cognition.[31]

I find it interesting that we talk about breathing as just something we do to exist. But what makes a difference is when we begin to pay attention to it.

Even elite military groups, such as Navy SEALs, use breath work to remain calm and maintain access to the prefrontal cortex when under stress. One popular technique is "box breathing," a quick and effective method. And it goes like this:

1. Sit comfortably with your feet on the floor. Relax your hands, fingers, jaw, and shoulders.
2. Inhale through your nose to a count of four; hold for four; then exhale through your nose for four, and hold again for four.
3. Repeat this cycle three times.

Reflecting Our Creator

Wim Hof, famously known as the Dutch "Iceman," has become a global figure for his remarkable feats of endurance. Known for climbing Mount Everest in only shorts and shoes and for running half-marathons on ice, Hof has amazed the world with his ability to push human limits. He shares his techniques with others through what he calls the *Wim Hof Method*.[32] He is widely credited with bringing the benefits of cold exposure, or "cold plunging," to mainstream awareness. His three-pillar method—conscious breathing, cold exposure, and commitment—offers a pathway to reconnect with nature and deepen self-awareness.

Hof claims his method can unlock a wide range of benefits, including increased energy, better sleep, reduced stress, heightened focus, stronger willpower, and a more resilient immune system. His teachings have spurred interest in scientific research, providing empirical evidence for his approach. A recent study by Jelle Zwaag et al found that combining Hof's breathing techniques with cold exposure may support the treatment of autoimmune diseases due to its anti-inflammatory effects.[33]

Whether gentle or extreme, the transformative effects of disciplined practices such as breath work, meditation, and movement are unmistakable. From people breaking through addiction to those seeing autoimmune disorders in the rearview mirror, the combination of commitment and the body's natural response powerfully reflects our Creator. Crafted in His image by the ultimate artist, our bodies are extraordinary and resilient—even in their fallen state.

I do not know whether Hof is a believer, but his methods raise a question that reaches beyond any one person. Many Christians may feel uncertain when they see people outside the faith experiencing transformation through practices like the Wim Hof Method. These practices often get dismissed as "New Age." But the meaningful, positive changes they bring shouldn't be discounted.

The Bible calls us to be vigilant, guarding against false teachings and spiritual deception to protect our faith in Jesus. But this caution raises an important question: Could we be using this vigilance as a shield, avoiding the responsibility to honor our bodies as temples in the way God designed? By not fully exploring the potential of our bodies and minds, are we limiting the greatness He has placed within us? Could we even be restricting what God might accomplish through us? And, in doing so, are we holding back the power He wants to reveal in our lives? Someday, will we have to answer for not fully embracing and honoring the incredible design He entrusted to us?

The word *power* traces its roots back to the Latin word *potere*, meaning "to be able." When we meditate on God's unlimited power, his unlimited ability, we can be reminded of who God is by what He's done for us.

When Jesus breathed His final breath, He saved us. The descent into despair and death was forever reversed. Through that last breath, Jesus brought forgiveness, freedom, and the promise of eternal life—gifts that changed the world forever. After His resurrection, Jesus breathed on His disciples (John 20:22) imparting the Holy Spirit. This act reassured them that they would never be left alone but would be empowered by God's presence within. While our physical bodies have limits, our souls and spirits can live fully, united with Christ, both now and for eternity.

When we meditate on the depth of God's power and love, we can set aside our ego, pride, and resistance, finding ourselves at Jesus's feet. Without Him, we carry an emptiness that only He can fill. No amount of effort or striving can replace that fullness. As Henry Nouwen put it, "God will offer you the deepest satisfaction you can desire."[34]

In His presence, we are filled, surrounded, and able to rest in His embrace. He calls to us as a friend: "Be still and know. Stop striving; let go of control. I will fight your battles. Sit with Me."

In Section 1, we explored how to love the Lord your God with all your heart. In this section, we focused on practices to renew our minds. As we prepare to transition to the next section, which explores loving God with all our soul, let's pause a moment and pray together:

> Lord, I ask that any disillusionment, confusion, stubbornness, worry, or despair be released from my being. Instead, fill me with a deep, true connection to You. Hear my voice as I speak and help me to discern Your voice in return. Guide me in ways that honor You, myself, and those around me. Fill me with Your joy, peace, confidence, and faith, drawing strength from You alone. Amen.

Now go into your week and let God's presence be the breath to your nostrils, the inhale to your heart, the exhale from your mind, and oxygen to your soul. With that, let's get into this week's exercises.

Activities Week 6

Heart (physical exercise): Upon waking, do child's pose with gratitude. Then do ten pushups against the wall or on the floor with or without knees on the floor.

Mind (cleanse): Perform box breathing for a few rounds.

Soul (renew and restore): Write down Isaiah 26:3: *"You will keep in perfect peace those whose minds are steadfast, because they trust in you"* (NIV). Each day, practice a prayer of *Unfolding Silence*—a prayer that gradually opens space for silence as words gently fall away. Engage in it as a meditation: Close your eyes, focus your breath, and repeat only a few words at a time, allowing them to diminish. Here's an example:

> "You will give peace. You will give peace.
> You will give. You will give.
> You will. You will.
> You."

Loving Others (scripture and prayer): Read Proverbs 3:5–6: "*Trust in the* LORD *with all your heart; do not depend on your own understanding. Seek his will in all you do and he will show you which path to take.*"

SECTION 3:

"Love the Lord your God with all your Soul"

CHAPTER 7:
FROM DARKNESS TO LIGHT

The most common form of despair is not being who you are.

—Soren Kierkegaard

My favorite high school teacher was Mr. Aase ("Ah-say"). His lessons blew my mind. He was an English teacher, outdoor enthusiast, avid bicyclist, proud Norwegian, father, and husband. In 2013, he passed away of pancreatic cancer at too young an age.

In Mr. Aase's class, we watched Pink Floyd's *The Wall*[35] and wrote an essay about our impressions. He gave us a pass on misspelled words if we drew a circle around them. After we read Naturalist writers, he took the class on a nature walk, and we identified trees; then he quizzed us on them while he projected images of trees on a whiteboard. In all these activities, he was our guide to mindfulness, and he made an impression on our souls.

But my favorite lesson was when Mr. Aase introduced us to Plato's *Allegory of the Cave*,[36] in which the main theme is a study of reality versus our perception of reality. Plato challenges how we as individuals respond when our perception of reality is confronted with true reality.

The philosophically important *Cave* allegory goes like this: Lifelong prisoners are chained to a wall inside a cave but facing a blank wall. Out of sight on the other side of the wall to which they are chained, objects pass in front of a fire creating shadows on the wall the men are facing. It's kind of like making shadow puppets with your hands in the dark. So, for their whole lives, the prisoners facing the blank wall have seen only shadows of images passing in front of them, not the direct source of the objects.

One day one of the men finally breaks out of his chains and heads outside the cave. His eyes have to adjust to the new light—sunlight, and he eventually comes to see a whole new world outside the cave. He returns to the cave with this new revelation. Of course, he wants his friends to be free and experience the sunlight too. But as his eyes adjust to the fire-lit cave, he is temporarily blinded. The other prisoners are proud of what they see and have always known. And they're seeing him weakened. So, they think that going outside the cave is harmful. Plato shares that since they assume this, they would kill anyone who tried to pull them outside the cave and into the sunlight, for fear of being harmed.

Mr. Aase aimed to instill in us teenagers a profound and authentic way of experiencing life—to look beyond the surface. This takes us back to where our journey in this book began, *Alice's Adventures in Wonderland*, which serves as a reminder that things aren't always what they seem.

Plato's Cave and a Life in Christ

As a follower of Jesus, I can't help but see Plato's allegory as a powerful metaphor for spiritual awakening and transformation. The cave and its darkness are our fallen world, a distorted mimic of what God intended His community to be. Seeing shadows in the dark cave is similar to the patterns of this world in which we are stuck, but we don't know it because we're blinded by sin. In our world, the people around us see and hear the same things we do, and that's comforting to us.

But Christ breaks our chains. And encountering Jesus opens our eyes to truth, freeing us from false beliefs. Our understanding grows, revealing life's true purpose. And even when met with resistance, we feel called to share Christ's light.

Plato's cave is a powerful analogy for moving from bondage to freedom—a journey deeply reflective of a life in Christ. In *The Truth and Beauty*, Andrew Klavan puts it this way: "When you see the world as it truly is, you begin to break out of the flow of its glorious illusions."[37]

Soul Versus Spirit

So far in this book we've discussed physical and mental exercises that nurture our body and our brain. Spiritual exercise of the soul takes a different approach to help us gain clarity and grow in self-awareness. Exercising the soul also builds a resilience in us to face life's challenges.

But what is our soul? And how is it different from our spirit? Are they the same thing? In exploring the Hebrew and Greek translations of the Old and New Testaments, I've come to believe they are not interchangeable. But the distinction is nuanced.

In *The Soul: How We Know It's Real and Why It Matters,* J. P. Moreland proposes a unique definition of the term *soul.* According to Moreland, the soul, or the Hebrew *nephesh,* represents the entire person—including our conscious thought, action, and emotion. And this concept is not limited to humans but also applies to animals and even God. The soul cannot be equated with physical breath or biological life alone. Instead, it holds intrinsic value that transcends physical processes. He also explains that "it's the soul of man that departs at life and returns at resurrection. It proceeds from and returns to God and that which gives human life."[38]

The spirit or the Hebrew *ruach,* which we learned about in an earlier chapter, signifies breath, which makes something animated, alive. And behind our spirit is a life force—a notion of power that gives us life and consciousness. God breathed His spirit into man at creation. So God's breath or spirit, *ruach,* animated the human soul, making man alive. And by so doing, He divinely connected Himself to us.

Our soul and spirit take an interconnected path from life to earthly death. And the Bible teaches us how this works: Our soul encompasses our entire being with our spirit serving as its life force. These are given to us when we are formed. And by practicing acts of self-awareness, we remain connected to the "Son," who is the Light of the World. As we live, the Holy Spirit continues to transform our spirit. When our time on earth comes to an end, our body becomes lifeless without the spirit, and our soul returns to God.

I believe the man who escapes the cave in Plato's allegory longs to live a life that reflects his innermost being. He is aware that his soul is starving. He courageously runs to the possibility of fulfillment, risking everything. When he encounters the light, his soul is nourished, and his spirit comes alive.

Let's look at the New Testament story of Saul who also came into his truest sense of self when he was blinded by light.

Saul's Spiritual Rebirth

Before his conversion, the Apostle Paul was a Jewish Pharisee, known as Saul, who viewed Christians as a threat to Jewish law and traditions. Acts 9:1 says, *"Saul was uttering threats with every breath and was eager to kill the Lord's followers."*

On his way to Damascus to chain up men and women who followed "the Way," Saul is suddenly surrounded by a blinding light from heaven. He falls to the ground, hearing the voice of Jesus asking, *"Saul, Saul, why are you persecuting me"* (Acts 9:4)? He gets himself up, but when he opens his eyes, he is blind. So his speechless companions lead him to Damascus where he stays for three days; he is blind and does not eat or drink anything (Acts 9:1–9).

During his period of fasting, we learn that he receives a vision about a man named Ananias coming to lay hands on him to restore his sight. And indeed, the Lord speaks a unique assignment to Ananias in a vision, telling him to go to Saul who is praying to God at that moment. There is a readiness within Saul, but Ananias is in disbelief. He tells God that he has heard about the terrible things that Saul has done to followers of Christ. God says to Ananias: *"Saul is my chosen instrument to take my message to the Gentiles and to kings, as well as to the people of Israel"* (Acts 9:15). So Ananias goes. He lays hands on Saul so that he *"might regain [his] sight and be filled with the Holy Spirit"* (Acts 9:17). Saul is baptized; then he eats food and regains his strength (Acts 9:10–19).

Saul's encounter with Jesus in a moment of intense, divine light contrasts sharply with the darkness he fell into immediately afterward. He was left physically blind to wrestle with the revelation he received. His blindness forced him to confront the spiritual darkness of his life up to that point. It revealed the depth of his need for transformation, and it marked the beginning of his new life as Paul, a passionate follower of Christ.

Fasting and Reflection

Many people do some version of fasting, which helps them lose weight and feel better. And I love it. In January 2023, I was led into a different kind of fasting, spiritual fasting. I grew up in the church, but I had no idea how to fast because no one talked about it. So, I read four books on fasting before beginning weekly twenty-four-hour fasts and three-day fasts every quarter. I found many of the answers I needed in Arthur Wallis's book, *God's Chosen Fast*;[39] it became my ultimate guide for spiritual fasting. Another helpful book is *The Daniel Fast* by Susan Gregory.[40]

The prompt to fast flowed from my 2023 "word for the year," which was *abide*. If you've never prayed over a word to guide your year, then I encourage you to do it. It's not something you conjure up on your own. You pray over it: "Lord God, show me a word you have specifically for me and the plans you have for me this year." And when the word is given to you, you know. And that word becomes the lens through which you see your experiences, ways, thoughts, and conversations. It changes you.

And year after year, the words you're given begin to integrate and sculpt you into the person you're becoming.

Jesus tells us in John 15:4–5 and 7:

> *Remain* [or abide] *in me, and I will remain in you. For a branch cannot produce fruit if it is severed from the vine, and you cannot be fruitful unless you remain in me. Yes, I am the vine; you are the branches. . . . Those who remain in me, and I in them, will produce much fruit. . . . But if you remain in me and my words remain in you, you may ask for anything you want, and it will be granted!*

After adopting my word for the year, I found myself drawn to the idea of fasting. It was a new opportunity to embark on a journey with God, one that would challenge and strengthen my faith.

No matter what kind of fasting you do, the results go deep. If we withhold food from ourselves, we're able to slough off the toxins in our body. We renew cells, increase our metabolic rate, regulate blood sugar, reduce inflammation, and support fat-burning. Our body goes through these processes because we are designed that way. We really have nothing to do with it. We make the decision to remove food, but we get all these benefits without having to do anything. It's actually a subtraction: no meal planning, spending money, fetching the food, prepping the food, taking the time to eat, or cleaning up dishes. I found Mindy Pelz's *Fast Like a Girl* to be helpful because it outlines the physical processes our bodies experience during fasting. It particularly focuses on optimal fasting timing for women, aligning practices with hormone levels for enhanced effectiveness.[41]

Our body is our temple, and these physical processes are a perfect translation into going soul deep. In spiritual fasting, the same thing is happening. God is chiseling out our character and revealing things to us. We enter a sacred space of quiet while going about our everyday duties. And we are more aware of our participation in the invisible struggle of this world—darkness and light as well as the natural instincts of the flesh and the spirit within. Fasting is a physical and spiritual reset.

When we fast, we're participating in some small way in Jesus's suffering. On this side of heaven, we will never wrap our heads around how God in all His magnificence sent His Son Jesus to us on earth. And through His struggle in His war against evil and in His ultimate victory, He reset the entire story of the world.

So when we spiritually fast, it's not because we must. Through the discipline of fasting, we can strip off every weight that slows us down, especially the sin that so easily trips us up. And with endurance, we can run the race God has set before us. We do this by keeping our eyes on Jesus the champion who initiates and perfects our faith. This divine discipline means He's treating us as His own children. And divine discipline is always good for us as we learn in the book of Hebrews, so that we can share in His holiness. When we train in this way, we are promised a peaceful harvest of righteous living afterward (Hebrews 12:1–6, 7, and 10b–11).

Saul's three-day fast was a time of humility and inner transformation, preparing him for a new purpose. By fasting he opened space to hear God's voice without distraction. Similarly, fasting today helps us quiet our lives and find spiritual clarity. It invites us to release control, just as Saul surrendered his plans and ego, creating room for God to work. Fasting also reminds us that true sustenance comes from God's presence rather than physical nourishment alone. It offers a unique pause to reconnect with God through prayer, the Word, and spiritual alignment.

The Ceremony of Baptism

When Paul was hiding out in Damascus for those three days, he was staying on Straight street in the house of a man named Judas (Acts 9:10–12). We know nothing about this man other than his hospitality. How would he have known that by opening his home, it would become the setting for Paul's dramatic spiritual rebirth? And everything that happened there marked the turning point for one of Christianity's most influential leaders.

God uses people to create futures and change lives. It was in Judas's home that one believer, Ananias, laid hands on Saul and baptized him. Three people—one significant moment. I imagine Ananias felt overcome by his active participation in what became a beautiful ceremony. By laying hands on Saul, he blessed him and commissioned him as a leader, and Paul was healed and filled him with the Holy Spirit. When Ananias baptized him, I wonder whether he poured water on his head from a pitcher, dunked him in a basin, or took him to a nearby creek? The Scripture doesn't say. What we do know is that Saul's heart was pierced, and he was moved to change. And we know at least two people were witnesses to this outward sign of his inward transformation. After Saul got up, we learn that he stayed with believers in Damascus for a few more days. Then he was ready to go: *"And immediately he began preaching about Jesus in the synagogues, saying, 'He is indeed the Son of God'"* (Acts 9:20).

Ceremonies, like baptism, are important, but cultural shifts in our modern world have made traditional ceremonies feel less significant. As more people identify as secular or "spiritual but not religious," traditional ceremonies like baptism often lose personal relevance. Without a shared belief system, the deep meaning and communal ties of these rituals don't always resonate. People are left searching for new ways to celebrate life's milestones in ways that feel true to their unique spiritual paths.

Yet baptism is an essential step in the life of a believer. Jesus Himself modeled it at the hand of his cousin John in the Jordan River (Matthew 3:13–17). Imagine standing in the sand watching this most talked about man in your world going down in the water to get baptized. And as He comes up out of the water, the sky opens up. Then you see the Spirit of God descending like a dove settling on Him, and you hear an audible voice from heaven say, *"This is my dearly loved Son, who brings me great joy"* (Matthew 3:17). It's one of the most beautiful moments in the Bible. And Jesus instructed us to do for others as his cousin did for Him, *"Go and make disciples of all the nations, baptizing them in the name of the Father and the Son and the Holy Spirit"* (Matthew 28:19).

Baptism is a personal act of faith. And like in Paul's story, it marks our commitment to follow Christ and join His family of believers.

Paul explains: *"For we died and were buried with Christ by baptism. And just as Christ was raised from the dead by the glorious power of the Father, now we also may live new lives"* (Romans 6:4). Baptism is more than a symbolic washing away of sins; it's a profound enactment of dying to the old self and being resurrected to a new self in Christ. It is a spiritual ceremony that encourages believers to live with the freedom and purpose that comes from that new life. Our separation from God is left behind. We are no longer bound by the past. We can embrace the identity and relationship with God made possible by Christ's resurrection. And in doing so in the community of other believers, we are supported in that spiritual rebirth and the journey that follows. In baptism, then, the journey from water to air is a metaphor for the spiritual journey from darkness to light. And stepping into life with Christ brings clarity, hope, and a newfound purpose that shines into every part of our lives.

Living As Light

We are called to live as lights in the world, embodying virtues like love, kindness, and integrity. As believers, we reflect divine light in a world that often feels dark. Our actions, choices, and interactions should mirror God's love and truth, serving as a beacon of hope and guidance for others. By living intentionally and embracing these virtues, we invite others to experience the light that comes from God and walk in His ways. It's a journey of growing in our understanding and relationship with Him.

Along this journey, interruptions in life offer valuable moments of self-reflection. These moments give us the opportunity to identify areas where we may be stuck or unaware of dysfunction. To truly see these areas clearly, we need God's Word to guide us. Hebrews 4:12 reminds us, *"For the word of God is living and active, sharper than any two-edged sword, piercing to the division of soul and spirit, of joints and marrow, and discerning the thoughts and intentions of the heart"* (ESV).

God's Word reveals the things in us that need change, helping us align with His purpose and see from His perspective. This allows us to move beyond distortion and act with wisdom and clarity.

As we make time each week to engage in spiritual exercises like reading God's Word, meditating, and praying, we deepen our relationship with Him. In doing so, we invite Him to examine our hearts, revealing emotions and thoughts we may have overlooked. As Dallas Willard puts it, our soul is "the aspect of our whole being that correlates, integrates, and enlivens everything going on in the various dimensions of the self."[42] Spending time with God awakens our soul and empowers us to release what holds us back, leading us on the right path. This practice cultivates self-awareness, which is essential for spiritual growth and transformation. By nurturing this awareness, we open ourselves to greater understanding, personal growth, and deeper connection with God.

We'll dive into looking at the patterns and designs of God in the next chapter. But before we do, let's get to this week's exercises.

Activities Week 7

Heart (physical exercise): Upon waking, do the child's pose with gratitude. Then, sit cross-legged on the floor or in a chair. Roll your head side to side five to eight times, stretching out your neck.

Mind (cleanse): What is one thing you can "fast" from this week? Think through how to free up space within yourself and your day by subtracting something. Maybe that will mean fasting from a type of food or a meal or from social media or TV.

Soul (restore and renew): Journal on your word for the year. If you don't have one, pray for God to reveal a "theme" word for you. If you have selected a word of the year, reflect on the experiences it has represented in your life.

Loving Others (scripture and prayer): Read the "abide in Me" (verses John 15:4–7). Then turn your thoughts to God and pray.

CHAPTER 8:
PATTERNS AND PURPOSE

The two most important days in your life are the day you are born and the day you find out why.

—Mark Twain

Imagine on a cool autumn morning, you step outside for a walk just as the sun is beginning to rise. Bundled up, you see mist hovering over a nearby creek. Golden light filters through the trees illuminating spider webs glistening with dew. You breathe in the crisp air, in awe of the careful details in the world around you. From the tiniest leaf to the vastness of the sky, everything feels perfectly placed. It's as though each element is there to create a masterpiece only visible in that single, fleeting moment.

You continue walking along the open trail and notice the subtle, yet consistent patterns woven into nature: the veins in a leaf mirroring the branches on the tree above, the spirals of a snail's shell, the way birds move in graceful unison. And it dawns on you that these designs aren't random. They are part of a larger, unseen order, woven together like a beautiful tapestry. It's the definition of harmony playing out all around you. Every part seems to know its place and purpose, as if guided by an invisible hand that understands and holds all things.

These reverent moments of beauty and the order in creation call to our souls. And we realize that just as the forest is filled with patterns and purpose, our lives too have meaning and direction. The harmony in those moments can be a reminder to trust in a greater plan. We can find inspiration and peace in the thought that we are a part of something far bigger than ourselves. And we can be gently reminded that our own journey, with its twists and turns, is connected to the wider rhythm of life.

Yes! God holds many mysteries beyond human understanding. But we can be certain of a few things. God is an intentional designer. He reveals patterns that shape not only the world around us but also transform our inner lives—our souls. His character and purpose are displayed through each aspect of His creation, His interactions with humanity, and His shaping of individual lives. And He is consistently faithful in equipping us with skill and filling us with the courage to act.

God's Equipping Power

Let's look at a man named Bezalel who was an artist and craftsman. His story shows how God intricately weaves His patterns and designs in the lives of His people to accomplish His purposes. Bezalel was chosen by God Himself to lead the construction of all the holy things God's people would be carrying with them while they traveled to the Promised Land (Exodus 31:1–5).

A couple months after the Israelites left Egypt, the backdrop of their lives was wild. Picture God's presence as a pillar of fire and a cloud leading them as they wandered, shrouding them with protection. When they camped out at Mount Sinai, they saw Moses and the leaders heading up the mountain to hear from God. Moses continued to climb higher into a cloud, which the people saw as flames. On Mount Sinai, Moses received specific instructions on what God wanted Him to build and how everything should look. From the Tabernacle and the Ark of the Covenant to the anointing oil to the utensils, the lavish materials and detailed designs used to create them symbolized God's beauty and holiness (Exodus 13:21–22; 19:25–31).

In Exodus 31:1–5, God tells Moses that He specifically selected Bezalel as the master craftsman for the job. God *"filled him with the Spirit of God, giving him wisdom, ability, and experience in all kinds of crafts"* to make artistic designs in gold, silver, and bronze; to cut gemstones; and to work with wood. God even appointed and gave special skills to an assistant for Bezalel and an entire team.

God didn't simply command that the Tabernacle be built; He provided Bezalel with the skills and inspiration needed to bring it to life. He wasn't chosen randomly; he was specifically called and gifted for this purpose. And whether Bezalel felt up for the task or not, he grabbed the baton and said yes.

And He's equipped you and me with a skill to be a part of the bigger picture of life. Maybe it's something you're really good at, maybe it's something you're interested in, or maybe it's something you've been doing for a long time. If it's not one of those cases, then you may be exploring. You may be wondering what God's will is for your life, or you may be going from thing to thing searching for His will. Or you may see and taste yourself in a role, but it feels years off from where you are.

Personality tests have a way of uncovering aspects of ourselves that often remain hidden in the blind spots of our self-perception. Assessments such as *StrengthsFinder*,[43] the *Enneagram*,[44] or *Seven Frequencies of Communication*[45] can act as mirrors, reflecting not only how we're wired but also how God has uniquely equipped us to contribute to His kingdom. They remind us that self-discovery is a journey, revealing layers of purpose and potential we may not have fully understood before.

Yet, as insightful as these tools can be, they only point to a deeper truth: God has already given us a clear picture of His will for our lives. It's not shrouded in mystery or dependent on a specific personality type. In 1 Thessalonians 5:16–18, He lays it out plainly: *"Always be joyful. Never stop praying. Be thankful in all circumstances, for this is God's will for you who belong to Christ Jesus."* These simple but profound instructions guide our attitudes and actions, shaping how we approach the unique gifts He's placed in us.

Understanding ourselves better through personality tools isn't just about self-awareness; it's about stewardship. When we align what we discover with God's will, we gain clarity on how to use our strengths to reflect His light, love, and truth in the world. Whether it's through creativity, leadership, empathy, or any other gift, living in gratitude, joy, and constant connection with God transforms self-discovery into divine purpose.

Sometimes, we lose sight of what we're equipped with because life gets so busy. When life became quieter during my bout with shingles, I found space to reflect. I started taking inventory of the activities I truly loved such as reading and writing. These had been hobbies of mine since childhood, but somewhere along the way, they got sidelined. Nurturing a marriage, having babies and raising them, building a business were worthy investments of time and energy, but in the stillness, I realized it was time for those passions to resurface.

Sometimes, we're not drawn to something until we get good at it, and then something shifts. Often, we begin with very little knowledge or confidence in a task, responsibility, or pursuit. That's where the crossroads appear. Decision points. It's where courage meets opportunity, and God's calling becomes undeniable. Yet, we must choose to say yes. We must move and take risks, even when they come at a cost.

Courage is essential in this space. It takes boldness to step out in faith and apply the talents God has placed within us—especially in areas where we feel unsure or unprepared. But God doesn't just equip us with skills and passions; He also equips us with the courage to use them. Just as He gifted Bezalel with artistry for building the tabernacle, He equips each of us with unique gifts that reflect His creativity and glory. The challenge—and the joy—is choosing to trust Him, stepping into those opportunities, and letting His purpose unfold through our obedience.

Opportunity and Courage Meet

Now let me tell you an outrageous story about two women with a whole lot of courage. One is a dark-haired wife and mom who carried a ton of responsibility as one of Israel's Old Testament judges. Not the kind of judge we know today. In those days, judges were unique and multifaceted leaders raised up by God to guide, deliver, and lead the Israelites during a turbulent period in their history. Judges were military or political figures seen as a manifestation of God's care and intervention. But they were also spiritual guides. This judge's name was Deborah. And her courage was rooted in a deep faith in God (Judges 4–5).

The other woman in this story is Jael. While we don't know much about her beyond the fact that she was married, one thing is clear: She carried a fierce, untamed fire within her. Though she doesn't have a long narrative in the Bible, her actions are unforgettable (Judges 4:17–22; celebrated in Judges 5:24–27).

Deborah was an answer to the prayers of her people who had been oppressed for twenty years by a King Jabin and his army commander Sisera. Jabin and Sisera. Picture the good guys in the movie Gladiator: Emperor Marcus Aurelius and army Commander Maximus, played by Russell Crowe. Now, picture the bad guy: Joaquin Phoenix's character, Commodus. King Jabin and Sisera were like him.

One day Deborah summons her army Commander Barak to the eponymous palm tree she sits beneath. She tells Barak to gather their warriors because that would be the day of victory. She says that God is going to deliver King Jabin's armies led by Sisera into the hands of the Israelites. Barak is nervous about going against these guys, but he agrees to go only if she goes with him.

Meanwhile, near the location where this battle is about to go down, sweet Jael and her husband Heber, who are descendants of Moses, had made a new home after moving away from their tribe. We'll come back to them in a minute.

Now Sisera gathers his chariots and warriors and heads to the designated battle site after hearing that Deborah, Barak, and their team are ready to fight. Deborah readies Barak and the warriors with her battle cry of encouragement: "Victory is yours; the Lord is marching ahead of you." They're filled with courage, and they attack! And not one of King Jabin's warriors is left alive, except Sisera himself, who flees on foot to the nearby tent of sweet Jael and Heber.

It turns out that Heber is friends with King Jabin. Aha . . . we have an inkling of why the couple may have moved away from their tribe. So now with Sisera's guard down, sweet Jael goes out to meet him, invites him in, gives him some milk to drink and puts a blanket over him. Sisera tells her to stand at the door and if anyone comes by to ask if someone is there, she is to say no. Now he can relax. All is quiet. He falls into a deep sleep from exhaustion.

But Jael, who is loyal to Deborah and her people tiptoes back in. She holds a hammer in one hand and tent peg in another, crouches down to where he is sleeping and lines up her tools with his temple. She takes a breath and then drives the tent peg into his head and the ground, killing him. Sweet Jael went savage—Stephen King style.

Awhile later, Deborah's right hand man Barak comes knocking on the door of the tent. He's on the hunt for Sisera. Jael walks him in to find Sisera lying dead with the peg through his temple. And in that moment Barak realizes their victory. In fact, following that event, we learn that the people of Israel only got stronger, and ultimately King Jabin was destroyed. This is a turning point in the history of God's people.

Two Kinds of Strength

Deborah and Jael are a profound picture of different kinds of strength: one as a steady guide and the other as an unexpected, decisive force. Two women called to different purposes to change the future. They remind us to embrace both everyday responsibility and extraordinary courage.

Deborah stands out as a true leader. She's wise, confident, and deeply connected to her purpose. She was a prophetess, a judge, and a warrior in her own right, guiding her people with clarity and strength. Unlike many leaders who sought power for their own gain, Deborah led with a servant's heart, prioritizing justice and her people's well-being. She was also able to inspire others. She didn't hesitate to call Barak to action, but when he wavered, she stepped into the fight alongside him. Deborah reminds us that good leadership is as much about courage and vision as it is about empowering others to rise to their potential.

And Jael was remarkably brave. She carried a quiet strength and rose to the occasion with courage and decisiveness when it mattered most. Her role in the story shows us that boldness doesn't always come from grand gestures or positions of authority. Sometimes, it's about standing firm in the moment you're given, even when it's dangerous or unexpected. She was decisive, resourceful, and fearless in dealing with Sisera, taking action where others might have hesitated. Courage can emerge from anyone, even in the most surprising circumstances.

Courage and Trust

Courage is a recurring thread in God's work, woven into the lives of those He calls to trust Him beyond their fears. It doesn't mean we won't feel afraid. It means choosing faith in God's presence, power, and purpose despite that fear.

One of my favorite quotes by Dan Sullivan is asked in the form of a question: "What's the difference between confidence and courage? Courage doesn't feel good."[46] When we practice being courageous time and time again, we become confident. And when our faith is grounded in God, we begin to trust Him more and more, despite the circumstances. This type of courage reflects God's character, which is faithful, constant, and ready to equip those who step forward in obedience.

Choosing courage shapes our souls. It deepens our faith and frees us from fear's grip. It aligns us with God's purposes, enabling us to face challenges with resilience and hope. As we trust in His strength, our courage reflects His beauty and reveals the greater pattern of His work—a pattern that transforms us and reveals His love to the world.

The Pattern of God's Beauty

God's love of beauty is evident in both the complexity and elegance of creation. In Genesis, we see the ordered beauty of the cosmos, a reflection of His divine design. And the creation of the Tabernacle at Bezalel's hands reveals God's intention for beauty in the spaces where His people encounter Him.

Beauty is central to how we connect with God. And the order of nature and the Tabernacle are examples of God's emphasis on beauty. They were designed to be visually stunning and filled with art, colors, and symbolism. God directed every detail, from the materials used to the way objects were arranged. These details were intended to reflect His holiness and beauty. For God, beauty isn't an afterthought; it's a part of His character and His design.

In the New Testament, we see God's beauty in the life of Jesus. He reflects the character of God perfectly (Hebrews 1:3); His interactions with people—healing the sick, forgiving the sinner, comforting the brokenhearted—are acts of beauty and restoration. This pattern reflects God's intention to restore His creation to wholeness.

God's beauty isn't merely aesthetic; it's a restorative power that transforms people. When we recognize God's beauty in creation, in others, and in His redemptive work, we are drawn into deeper worship. We also begin to reflect that beauty ourselves, living in a way that points back to the Creator.

Redemption: God's Grand Design

The ultimate pattern in the Bible is the story of redemption. It's a theme that weaves through every book and culminates in Jesus Christ. From the moment sin entered the world, God set a plan in motion to redeem humanity. The Old Testament provides glimpses of this redemption through stories of deliverance, sacrifices, and covenants. Each story points forward to a greater fulfillment in Jesus.

Jesus is the embodiment of God's redemptive plan. His life, ministry, death, and resurrection fulfill the promises made throughout the Old Testament. In Him, we see God's desire to restore all things. Jesus's sacrifice on the cross is the ultimate act of forgiveness, making it possible for us to be reconciled to God. This act is not isolated; it is part of a grand design that spans history. By returning to God and placing our faith in

Jesus, we are invited into a restored relationship with God and a life that reflects His purposes.

And the pattern of redemption is alive and well today. God continues His work of restoring the lives of believers today. Through the Holy Spirit, we are being transformed and shaped to reflect Jesus more fully. This process, called sanctification, is part of God's design for each believer. Just as He crafted the Tabernacle, equipped Bezalel, and gave courage to Deborah and Jael, God shapes our lives with purpose, preparing us for His work.

Two Ways to Live Out God's Design Today

Recognizing God's patterns and designs in the Bible calls us to live out God's design by living with intentionality. When we understand that God is the designer who equips us, values beauty, and is faithful to His promises, we can approach life with a sense of purpose and trust. We see God's desire to draw humanity to Himself, transforming lives and communities. Embracing God's patterns means aligning our lives with His purposes.

We can live as reflections of His love and participate in His work of redemption. When we walk in these patterns, we are reminded of God's ultimate design: to restore all things through Jesus Christ. In Him, we find the fulfillment of every promise, the embodiment of God's beauty, and the assurance of His faithfulness. When we live in the light of these truths, we are empowered to live lives that honor God, reflect His character, and bring hope to the world.

Second, we live out God's design by internalizing His faithfulness. This is how He teaches our souls to trust. This is how we practice courage. This trust builds resilience within us even in times of uncertainty. Our soul can rest in God's promises. And a trusting soul finds peace in God's constancy. We are confident He will not abandon us, even if we feel He is far away from us.

God's intricate patterns of creation, redemption, and beauty remind us that His design transcends our understanding and circumstances. Even when life is overwhelming, His faithfulness remains steadfast. This is the foundation upon which we build our faith. It's where we trust not in our own ability to overcome, but in who God is and His power to restore and redeem. When we're faced with life's greatest challenges, we're called to rise above, not by relying on our own strength, but by leaning deeper into His presence. This leads us into the next chapter, where we will explore "The Yet Theory." It's a call to trust in God's sovereignty, even amid life's darkest moments, and to rise in faith despite the storms surrounding us.

Activities Week 8

Heart (physical exercise): Upon waking, do the child's pose with gratitude.

Mind (cleanse): Do round 2 of "Wake up, Shake up." Stand up. For twenty to thirty seconds, shake out your legs and feet, hips, arms and hands, and head. Then hold your stance and breathe for a few breaths.

Soul (restore and renew): Reflect on a time you acted boldly and stepped into courage. Is there a pending opportunity for you to do that again? Write it down.

Loving Others (scripture and prayer): Read Psalm 19:1–4:

The heavens proclaim the glory of God. The skies display his craftsmanship. Day after day they continue to speak; night after night they make him known. They speak without a sound or word; their voice is never heard. Yet their message has gone throughout the earth, and their words to all the world.

CHAPTER 9:
THE YET THEORY

The soul becomes dyed with the color of its thoughts.
—Marcus Aurelius

"It Is Well with My Soul"[47] is an old hymn, familiar to many who grew up in the church. But what isn't as well-known is the tragic backstory behind it.

In the 1800s, Horatio Spafford and his wife Anna have four daughters and a son. They lose their son to pneumonia in 1871, and Horatio, a lawyer and businessman faces financial disaster the same year after the Chicago Fire. In the aftermath, he gets his business up and running again. Then in 1873 he wants them all to sail the Atlantic on a trip to Europe. Unexpectedly, he has to handle some business dealings, so he sends Anna and the girls ahead; he would sail a few days after them.

On the way, their ship collides with another, and all four daughters die. Only Anna his wife survives; she is found floating on a piece of debris and is saved. She arrives in Europe and telegraphs the bad news to her husband. So he sails on the next available ship to be with his grieving wife. On that journey the captain points out to him the place where his daughters slipped into the depths of the Atlantic. It was then that Spafford was inspired to write these words:

> "Where peace like a river attendeth my way,
> When sorrows like sea billows roll,
> Whatever my lot, Thou has taught me to say,
> It is well, it is well with my soul."

Anna and Horatio Spafford went on to have three more children. But I have questions. Where did they get their strength to keep going? How could they continue in this life carrying the weight of their great loss? Never in this lifetime would they understand why this tragedy happened. Rather, it would seem, understandably, **not** well with their souls. Not one bit.

The Maturing of Faith

In times of deep emotional turmoil, we feel fragmented and yearn for a way out. Our minds spiral. We don't know what to do with ourselves and don't know how we can move forward.

Horatio Spafford experienced profound agony and sorrow, yet he wrote the paradoxical phrase, "It is well with my soul."

The wisdom of Proverbs 18:14 tells us, "*The human spirit can endure a sick body, but who can bear a crushed spirit?*" But people do; we see it all the time. The resilience of the human spirit fascinates me.

A few years ago my friend Jessica delivered a stillborn, Caden. She recently shared with our prayer group her state of disconnectedness afterward. Jessica's body continued to produce milk, but there was no baby. Her body thought there was, but her soul knew there wasn't. She and her husband's spirits were crushed, and their lives were changed forever.

One of the strongest souls I know is my mom's best friend Barbara. Her strength of spirit is evident to everyone that knows her. Her husband had a heart attack and died while he was driving them across country—to her son's funeral. He drove their RV right off a cliff where she clung for her life, climbing up the side of a mountain, bruised and broken waiting for help. She recuperated in a hospital for months afterward grieving both her husband and son.

We all know tragic stories like these even if we have not experienced them ourselves. The question in Proverbs remains, *"Who can bear a crushed spirit?"*

Horatio and Anna, Jessica, and Barbara all had one thing in common: their investment of time spent with God—knowing Him, what He said and what He did—paid dividends. They didn't cram positive words and ideas in their moments of grief. No, each of them had a faith built over many years and many struggles. They learned and experienced over time that Jesus was someone who could be trusted in all their circumstances. Their spirits were transformed by God's power and love so that in their weakness, they knew it and felt His Spirit strong in and around them.

Finding Meaning in Life

The book of Ecclesiastes was written by King Solomon, the wisest man who ever lived. In it he offers hard-earned wisdom. This is not the youthful, celebratory Solomon; it's the older, reflective king. The word *ecclesiastes* is the Greek translation of the Hebrew word *Qoheleth*, meaning one who convenes an assembly.[48] The book of Ecclesiastes is a series of reflections from *"the Teacher, King David's son, who ruled in Jerusalem"* (Ecclesiastes 1:1). And his words are sobering, even heavy, as he examines life's unfairness, injustice, and seeming lack of purpose. *"Everything is meaningless,"* Solomon repeats time and time again.

Ecclesiastes doesn't shy away from life's darker truths: oppression thrives, courts are corrupt, and wisdom doesn't guarantee a better fate. Whether one is wise, foolish, or mad, we all share the same end. Yet, amidst these grim observations, Solomon intersperses timeless insights that shed light on how to live meaningfully despite life's uncertainty. He offers wisdom for life, touching on everything from finances to relationships. In Ecclesiastes, he reveals ten powerful keys to unlocking meaning in everyday life:

- On handling money wisely: Give generously, for your gifts will return to you later. . . and diversify your investments (11:1–2, paraphrased).
- When it comes to youth, he encourages living with intention: *"Refuse to worry, and keep your body healthy."* (11:10). *"Don't let the excitement of youth cause you to forget your Creator"* (12:1).
- On the value of relationships, he reminds us, *"Two people are better off than one, for they can help each other succeed. If one falls, the other can reach out and help"* (4:9–10).
- Within his reflections on life's futility, Solomon finds meaning in embracing the present. He urges us to do our best in all we undertake: *"Whatever you do, do well"* (9:10).

- He advises contentment: *"Enjoy what you have rather than desiring what you don't have"* (6:9a).
- Above all, he emphasizes the importance of gratitude, declaring, *"There is nothing better than to be happy and enjoy ourselves as long as we can"* (3:12).
- Acknowledging the fleeting and unpredictable nature of life, Solomon observes, *"Just as you cannot understand the path of the wind or the mystery of a tiny baby growing in its mother's womb, so you cannot understand the activity of God, who does all things."* (11:5). Accept the mystery of life.
- His advice is to keep sowing seeds—both metaphorically and literally—because we can never know which efforts will bear fruit (11:6, paraphrased).
- Despite life's uncertainties and injustices, Solomon concludes that true meaning is not found in external circumstances but in centering our lives on God. He reminds us to embrace both the joys and challenges of life, saying, *"Enjoy prosperity while you can, but when hard times strike, realize that both come from God. Remember that nothing is certain in this life."* (7:14).
- He also celebrates the simple pleasures as divine gifts: *"I decided there is nothing better than to enjoy food and drink and to find satisfaction in work. Then I realized that these pleasures are from the hand of God"* (2:24).

The book of Ecclesiastes doesn't promise an easy life, but it offers profound truths about living well. While viewed through an earthly lens, life may feel meaningless. However, we are invited to anchor ourselves in God, who is the ultimate source of purpose.

A life well lived, per the wisest man on earth, can be distilled into the following: Work diligently, enjoy the simple pleasures, and seek joy in the moment. Respect God, follow His ways, and trust that He holds the ultimate plan. The book of Ecclesiastes teaches us that life's meaning isn't handed to us; it's created when we live with wisdom, gratitude, and faith.

Thankfulness: Our Sacrifice

True thankfulness often grows out of the soil of sacrifice. Horatio Spafford's story illustrates this connection powerfully. After losing his son, his wealth, and his daughters, he didn't immediately proclaim, "It is well with my soul." Instead, throughout his life he chose, moment by moment, to turn his heart toward God. Through his pain and questions of "Why me? Why them? Why this?" he remained in the struggle with God. This struggle, this deliberate turning toward the Light, is the essence of sacrifice.

Thankfulness becomes a sacrifice when it costs something and comes from faith in God's character during trials, not when it emerges from abundance and comfort. Choosing to be grateful in pain or uncertainty involves turning away from self-pity or bitterness and aligning ourselves with God's eternal goodness. It's a way of acknowledging Him as sovereign and faithful, even when circumstances might suggest otherwise. Psalm 34:18 reminds us that *"the Lord is close to the brokenhearted; he rescues those whose spirits are crushed."* This closeness is the gift that emerges from the cost of our surrender.

When we declare trust and don't deny our suffering, thankfulness occurs. By staying in the struggle with Jesus, even when it's hard, we move closer to the Light of the World. And through that sacrifice, thankfulness becomes a profound act of faith. It's a choice to trust that God is good, even when life is not. In the Bible, thankfulness is more than a feeling; it's an act of worship. It's a discipline of the heart. And in many ways, it's a spiritual offering that honors God. The Yet Theory shifts our focus from our circumstances to who God is, anchoring our hope in His promises.

The Yet Theory

Spiritual formation happens in our everyday moments. It unfolds over our lifetime. Dallas Willard explains that "spiritual transformation is a process of bringing all the parts of the person together. The soul is the unity of these dimensions."[49] And through this process, we can "bring the soul into harmony with what God is doing."[50]

And this is where what I call "The Yet Theory" becomes possible:

- It's that strange paradox of feeling disillusioned, yet . . . we can call on the Father, rest in His arms, and be under His protection. And He supernaturally gives it.
- It's a tragic human circumstance experienced, yet . . . we can trust the same power that raised Jesus from the dead be given to us. And He supernaturally gives it.
- The world is falling apart around you, yet . . . we can count on the Father's enduring faithfulness to us to be our enduring faithfulness in Him. And He supernaturally gives it.

All these supernatural abilities are wrapped into one word: hope. It's a hope rooted in what's to come—eternal life—where no pain, no confusion, no anger, no sadness, no loss, no grief exists. Where no part of us can feel disconnected, but we are fully whole, living in and with Jesus in peace. Remarkably, this same peace is available to us in the here and now, empowering us to live supernaturally in the natural world.

Yes, even in the here and now, we can rest assured that God's Spirit dwells within us. Though we may not understand the "whats" or "whys," we trust that His plans are good. We know our woes are temporary as we pass through life on earth in our broken state. This is the essence of living Proverbs 3:5: *"Trust in the Lord with all your heart; do not depend on your own understanding."*

The Yet Theory comes alive when we remember God. It's where faith enters the room. Faith takes hold of our hearts when we pray:

> Lord, give me trust in you. I want your Spirit in me. Open my heart and teach me your ways. Grow my faith. Thank you that in my pain, you are the "Yet." Please wrap me in the promise of your strength, endurance, and hope.

Remember

The thing about pain is this: It will all be okay. Whatever you're going through . . . It will all be okay. How can I be so certain in telling you this?

I recently prayed this question to God while dealing with a tough time with my teen. As I was journaling, I realized I was at my end. I couldn't fix what we were dealing with, try as I might.

I opened my Bible, and the page fell open to a Psalm. I was pretty astonished with how God answered me. In the Spirit, I heard:

> It will all be okay, not because you know what to do (I didn't). Not because you are strong (I was falling apart). Not because you aren't angry (I was!). Not because you are or are not doing spiritual things like praying, worshiping, fasting (I was). Not because your current circumstances are in a peaceful state (they were not). It came down to one thing and one thing only. It would all be okay because of WHO God is.
>
> So, I ask: Who are you, God?

He pointed me to these truths in Scripture:

> I'm One who does many acts of kindness (Psalm 106:7b).
> I'm One who saves and rescues (Psalm 106:4c, 10a).
> I'm One who holds mighty power (Psalm 106:8c).
> I'm One who counsels (Psalm 106:13c).
> I'm One who promises and carries through (Psalm 106:12a, 45a).
> I'm One who is patient (Psalm 106:14b).
> I'm One who is glorious (Psalm 106:2).
> I'm One who does wonderful and great things (Psalm 106:22).

I'm One who pities you (Psalm 106:44a).

I'm One who hears your cries (Psalm 106:44b).

I'm One who remembers my promises to you (Psalm 106:45a).

I'm One who loves you unfailingly (Psalm 106:45b).

I'm One who relents on my anger (Psalm106:45b).

I'm One who causes your oppressors to treat you with kindness (Psalm 106:46).

I'm One who gathers you (Psalm 107:3).

I'm One who is everlasting (Psalm 106:48).

I'm One who saves you from your distress (Psalm 107:6, 13, 19, 28).

I'm One who saves you from death (Psalm 107:20b).

I'm One who heals you by my word (Psalm 107:20a).

I'm One who is Jesus, the champion (Hebrews 12:2).

I'm One who is a warrior and fights on your behalf. (Exodus 15:3/Deuteronomy 3:22)

I'm One who satisfies your thirst. (Psalm 107:9a)

I'm One who fills the angry with good things. (Psalm 107:9)

I'm One who initiates and perfects your faith. (Hebrews 12:2)

I'm One who calms the storm in your life. (Psalm 107:29)

I'm One who breaks down your prison gates. (Psalm 107:16)

When I didn't know what else to do, all I needed was to *remember*. To go back to what He's done in the Bible for others and what He's done in my own life. Remember. Throughout the Bible, He tells us to remember. And He tells us to teach others to remember too because we easily get caught up in our own ways, our own strengths, our own self-centeredness. We forget about Him. Ultimately, it will all be okay, not because of you, but because of who.

Clouds: God's Presence

In the last chapter, I mentioned the cloud that cloaked God's people as they wandered through the wilderness in the book of Exodus. This imagery challenges our usual associations with clouds, transforming them into something profound and hopeful.

The Israelites felt frustrated, aimless, impatient, and afraid, yet the cloud was a reminder that God was with them. In this story the cloud offered reassurance and purpose even in their uncertainty.

Exodus 40:36–38 describes this beautifully:

> *Now whenever the cloud lifted from the Tabernacle, the people of Israel would set out on their journey, following it. But if the cloud did not rise, they remained where they were until it lifted. The cloud of the LORD hovered over the Tabernacle during the day, and at night fire glowed inside the cloud so the whole family of Israel could see it. This continued throughout their journeys.*

The cloud wasn't a sign of doom or despair. It was a sign of God's guidance, direction, and His constant presence, even when the path forward felt unclear. It was a constant and tangible sign that He had not abandoned His people.

This idea reminds me of a concept in Benjamin Hardy and Dan Sullivan's book, *The Gap and the Gain*[51] in which they explain how we can frame every experience as an opportunity for growth and learning—the gain. When we focus on what we've gained, we find meaning and perspective, no matter how difficult the circumstances. In contrast, dwelling on what we lack or what's not going right keeps us in the gap, fostering frustration, disappointment, and unhappiness.

I applied this mindset during the challenging season with my teenage son. It felt like a relentless storm—heavy clouds that wouldn't lift, with relentless wind and rain. But as I reflected on the Exodus story, I realized I could flip the symbol of the cloud on its head. Instead of viewing it as a sign of struggle, I saw it as a symbol of guidance, connection, and growth.

This shift in perspective allowed me to approach the situation with a renewed outlook as a mom. I could connect with my son more deeply, not despite the storm, but because of it. The cloud became a reminder that God's presence was with us both, guiding us through the wilderness together.

Sit with Me

One afternoon, a little while after our storm had passed, I sat with my son in his room, watching him play a video game. Headset on, he was deep in conversation with his friend Rob, who was also playing from his room. I simply wanted to be with my son. I had to put aside my initial "mom thoughts" as I scanned the mess: empty Gatorade bottles, clothes scattered on the floor, shoes left out of place. Thoughts raced through my mind: Why hasn't he cleaned this up? Is that computer screen turning his brain to mush? Why isn't he outside getting some fresh air?

I pushed my thoughts aside and chose connection. I asked him about his avatar—a falcon. He let me wear his headset so I could hear the music he played while gaming. I even chatted with his friend Rob. He explained to me how he scored points and navigated between worlds.

For many of you, the connection between your everyday life, whether filled with routine tasks or heavy challenges, and your spiritual world might feel unclear. Yet, by reading up to this point, I suspect that you sense, on some level, that these parts of life are connected. I'm convinced they are. We are spiritual beings navigating a material world, and a larger story is unfolding. In this story, God desires to meet us exactly where we are—messy rooms, chaotic days, painful circumstances and all. He's not waiting for us to tidy up our lives first. He simply wants to be with us, like a loving parent sitting beside their child in the "game" of life.

Jesus knows you. He sees you. And all of Heaven celebrates when you deal with the inevitable pains of life yet, remember Him. I believe God's ultimate desire is to draw all His children to Him, longing for reconciliation when all else fades away. He yearns for us to seek Him during our time on earth, offering His presence as a source of peace and strength.

By now, it's clear that the soul is the part of us that connects all the other parts. It's the space where God's Spirit meets us, where His presence reshapes us, and where He simply wants our broken spirits and our hearts.

And this is the invitation: to be with Him. To let Him sit with you. And when you do, the Holy Spirit begins to work, molding the invisible clay of your spirit. As you yield to this process, you'll experience peace that saturates every part of your mind, body, and soul. It's a rebirth—a realization that you're part of something far greater than yourself. In union with the

One who made you, you begin to shine with His light, reflecting His love in and around you.

With this chapter, we conclude our exploration of loving God with all our soul. Now we move forward to what Jesus calls the greatest instruction: to love others as we love ourselves. In this next section, we'll see how God's order applies to the ways we love and are loved, and we'll explore how this love can transform our world. Let's pause here and get to this week's activities before we go any further.

Activities Week 9

Heart (physical exercise): Upon waking, do the child's pose with gratitude. Then, do the bridge pose. Lie on your back with knees bent and feet flat on the floor. Arms are at your side with palms turned down. Make sure your shoulders are walked far away from your ears. Lift your hips up to the ceiling, peeling your spine off the floor, then slowly release down. Repeat five to eight times.

Mind (cleanse): Do round 2 of box breathing. Sit comfortably with your feet on the floor. Relax your hands, fingers, jaw, and shoulder; then inhale through your nose to a count of four and hold for four; then exhale through your nose for four, and hold again for four. Repeat three times.

Soul (restore and renew): Reflect on a circumstance in which you can use The Yet Theory, calling on God to wrap you in the promise of His strength, endurance, and hope.

Loving Others: Read Psalm 34 out loud each day this week. Let it be your prayer.

SECTION 4:

"Love Your Neighbor as Yourself"

CHAPTER 10:
THE WONDER OF LOVE AND OUR RELATIONAL DESIGN

It is not where you go in life, but who you travel with that matters.

— Charles M. Schulz

My son's sixth-grade biology assignment taught me a substantial spiritual lesson. He was asked to fill in a diagram's layers, starting with the smallest unit of life: the cell. Then he built outward: cells to tissues, tissues to the human body, the human body to family, family to community, and eventually to the city and the world. As we talked about it, I realized this was a perfect representation of our unity with the people with whom we share life on earth. It also highlighted an important truth: Each of us carries individual responsibility, not just for ourselves but for the integrity of the whole.

Unless we care for ourselves as individual organisms, the larger "net" cast out from us—our relationships, communities, and the world—will lack strength and integrity. In other words, we're only as strong as the individuals who make up the whole. We are made to serve the life and health of our communities, and to that end, each individual plays a vital role. That's been the focus of this book: nurturing the health of your individual body, mind, and soul and knowing that you have power, rooted and established in God's love for you.

Now, it's time to expand that focus. The journey inward was never meant to end there. It was preparing us for something greater: loving others. This section will explore what it means to be part of this greater whole. We'll move outward and uncover how our identity is shaped by our relationships and discover what it means to belong to the body of Christ, the church. Together, we'll reflect on the strength and unity found in God's design for His people and what it looks like to love others as we've been loved by Him. Let's step forward into the heart of what it means to love.

When Loving Others Feels Difficult

Many of our relationships are tough or broken. We can spend a lot of our time wondering how best to navigate situations between them. We ruminate on conversations or interactions that didn't go well, feeling misunderstood, betrayed, angry, hurt, and sometimes wondering why we left the house at all and why we have to be around others.

Have you seen those hats and T-shirts that say, "I like my dogs and maybe three people?" They're funny because we can all relate. Sometimes, it feels easier to isolate ourselves, shutting out people we don't want to deal with anymore. Depending on our experiences with someone, we might even harbor anger or resentment, entertaining dark, yet oddly satisfying, thoughts about their impending demise. That's exactly why God's instruction to "love your neighbor" is so essential. It's easy to love the ones who love us back, but loving the ones who don't? That's where the real challenge lies.

But He offers us His perspective in relationships. He reminds us that He loves and forgives even those we see as enemies. He calls us to rise above, to live with grace among others, and equips us with the strength to keep learning and growing in our failures, forgiving others and ourselves, and moving forward in peace.

In Search of Our Identity

You've heard it said that we are social creatures. According to a June 2022 article in *Neuroscience News*, social isolation is linked to changes in brain structure and cognitive deficits. Prolonged isolation can even increase the risk of developing dementia as we age.[52] Whether due to choice or circumstance, when we retreat from others, the impact on our minds and bodies is considerable. It's not just emotional; it's biological. And because our bodies are temples, designed to house the Spirit and reflect God's glory, this retreat affects us spiritually as well.

But why is that? Why are we so deeply wired for connection that being alone can impact us in such dramatic ways? To answer this, we need to go back to the beginning of things, examining our relational selves through both a scientific and spiritual lens. Let's journey into a fascinating theory that sheds some light on this. But before we get into the science, let me share the piece of art that sparked my thoughts about it all.

I first encountered Salvador Dali's 1931 painting, *The Persistence of Memory*, in high school. The melting clocks, blending softness and hardness, fullness and emptiness captivated me. Years later, visiting the Salvador Dalí Museum in St. Petersburg, Florida, I saw the masterpiece in person, and it came to life for me. Art critics have speculated that the painting connects to quantum mechanics, though Dalí denied it. I was intrigued, so I explored quantum physics just enough to understand its powerful implications. Carlo Rovelli's book *Reality Is Not What It Seems* describes quantum mechanics as a relational science; it reveals that the universe is not a collection of isolated things but a web of interactions.[53]

At its heart, quantum mechanics tells us that identity exists—whether of a particle, a plant, or a person—only in relation to something else. The universe functions through observation, measurement, and interaction. This isn't just science; it's a mirror of spiritual truth. Our world is built on relationships, pointing us to the ultimate relationship: our connection to God and one another.

The spiritual applications of the idea that we live in a participatory universe are far-reaching. One thing only has its identity in relation to its interaction with something else. This relational truth reflects not only the fabric of the cosmos but also the heart of our faith: Our identity is known through our Creator and through the relationships He designed us for.

The Design of Relationship: Unveiling the Trinity

To better understand our own identity, we must look to the Holy Trinity: Father, Son, and Holy Spirit. Three persons in one God.

The Trinity stands as one of the most unfathomable mysteries of all time. But I really believe that by taking a closer look at the roles of each person in the Godhead, we can better understand how our most important relationships work here on earth.

Jesus, the Son, is the simplest place to start unraveling this mystery because He came to earth as one of us, fully human. And also fully divine. People laid eyes on Him, touched Him, were healed by Him, and hugged Him. He fulfilled prophecies as the Messiah, which is derived from the Hebrew word *Mashiach*, or the Greek word *Christos*, both meaning "the anointed one".[54] He accepted and elevated the overlooked and revolutionized culture forever. Through His words, miracles, and resurrection, Jesus has inspired generations all over the world to love boldly, serve selflessly, and live with the freedom of knowing that nothing can hold you back.

Yet, Jesus never acted alone. Everything He did was part of the Father's plan, carried out through the power of the Spirit. Each person of the Trinity points to the other in perfect unity.

Jesus Himself said, *"Anyone who has seen me has seen the Father"* (John 14:9)!

The Father is the source of every good thing in our lives. Ephesians 1:3 puts it this way: *"All praise to God, the Father of our Lord Jesus Christ, who has blessed us with every spiritual blessing in the heavenly realms because we are united with Christ."*

The Spirit is our guide, the one who shows us the truth, convicts us when we stray, and gives us the strength to live out our faith. Jesus explained it in John 16:8: *"And when he* [the Spirit] *comes, he will convict the world of its sin, and of God's righteousness, and of the coming judgment."* In John 14:16, Jesus said, *"And I will ask the Father, and he will give you another Advocate* [or Comforter, Encourager, or Counselor] *who will never leave you."*

Yet, God's ultimate purpose is not to condemn but to save. As John 3:17 reminds us, *"God sent his Son into the world not to judge the world, but to save the world through him."* This shows us the heart of the Trinity—a God who works together as one to love, guide, bring truth and grace, and redeem us.

This divine relational design has meaningful implications for how we live. The Trinity models perfect love, interdependence, and unity. The Father sustains and wills, the Son redeems and serves, and the Spirit fills us and connects us. Each has a unique role, yet they are one in purpose.

How the Trinity Shapes Our Relationships

Reflecting on this mystery reveals the blueprint for our most important relationships, including marriage and family. Relationships thrive when we, like the Trinity, work in unity while respecting individual roles. Each person in the Holy Trinity—Father, Son, and Holy Spirit—points to the other.

We've previously discussed that the thing most valuable to God is us. This is our story. God came, He died, He lives. He will come again. And it's all for us. We look to Him, and we are saved. His kingdom is ours now and forever. The whole thing is a mystery and wonder. We will never fully get our heads wrapped around it while in our fallen state, but one day, we will fully know. And yet, we can understand our relationships with ourselves and with those around us better by connecting with the persons who make up the Trinity. Pretty amazing.

Let's take a closer look at two of those relationships: marriage and the bond between parent and child.

The person you marry probably has more influence on your spiritual journey than any other person on this earth. Two become one. It reminds me of the natural harmony expressed in yin and yang from Chinese philosophy. Yin, often associated with the feminine, symbolizes the moon, softness, darkness; while yang, representing the masculine, is linked to the sun, strength, and light. They are separate yet integral parts of the unified whole—each equally valuable and essential to balance and completeness.

In *Flow*, Mihaly Csikszentmihalyi shares these thoughts about relationships:

> To be enjoyable, a relationship must become more complex. To become more complex, the partners must discover new potentialities in themselves and in each other. To discover these, they must invest attention in each other, so that they can learn what thoughts and feelings, what dreams reside in their partner's mind. This in itself is a never-ending process, a lifetime's task.[55]

The back and forth, the ebb and flow, the commitment of two growing independently yet as one, and the freedom that comes within the responsibility of the relationship is a beautiful thing. One partner points to the other not with contempt, pride, or superficiality, but with love, respect, and sincerity.

And we can better understand the roles of a family through the lens of the Holy Trinity, particularly in the parent-child relationship. Henry Nouwen explores this beautifully in his bestselling book, *The Return of the Prodigal Son: A Story of Homecoming*.[56] Inspired by Rembrandt's famous painting of the biblical parable, Nouwen dives deep into the themes of the artwork and the story, reflecting on them in meditation. He is captivated by both the painting and the artist. And he takes readers on a journey of self-discovery and spiritual reflection. At first, he relates to the older son—the one who stayed obedient, towed the line, and didn't squander his inheritance. As an older brother himself, this was a natural connection. But as Nouwen reflects further, he begins to see himself in the wayward younger son, who falls before his father in repentance after living recklessly and descending into poverty and despair, desperately hoping for forgiveness.

As a Catholic priest, Nouwen also connects with the father figure in the parable and the painting. Rembrandt portrays the father with striking symbolism: one hand is soft and tender, like a mother's hand, and the other strong and firm, reflecting a father's protective strength. These details emphasize both the nurturing and guiding aspects of God's love, which are perfectly unified in the Holy Trinity.

Ultimately, Nouwen discovers that both the parable and the painting lead to the same conclusion: God, our Father, is always waiting with open arms to welcome us home. No matter what we've done or where we've been, His love and tenderness are steadfast, inviting us back into His embrace.

The Holy Spirit, Jesus, and the Father exist in perfect union. This is the Trinity. And through this divine relationship, we too are joined, united, and yoked with God. As Jesus says in John 14:20, *"I am in my Father, and you are in me, and I am in you."*

This incredible truth reveals that we are deeply connected to God, and He is always present within us.

Connecting to God

John Ortberg and Ruth Haley Barton describe seven unique ways people naturally connect with God in *The Ordinary Day with Jesus*.[57] These are called spiritual pathways. These pathways emphasize that each person has a unique way of connecting with God and growing spiritually, based on their personality, experiences, and natural inclinations. Most people find themselves drawn to one or two pathways, but exploring them all can deepen your spiritual life. Here's a rundown of the seven pathways:

- **Intellectual:** You connect with God best through learning, studying Scripture, and discovering new truths about Him.
- **Relational:** You feel closest to God when engaging with others in meaningful conversations or shared faith experiences.
- **Serving:** You encounter God through acts of service, helping others, and making a difference in practical ways.
- **Worship:** You experience God's presence through music, prayer, and moments of heartfelt praise.
- **Activist:** You sense God's purpose when working for justice, championing causes, or standing up for what's right.
- **Contemplative:** You find God in silence, solitude, and quiet reflection, connecting through prayer and stillness.
- **Creation:** You feel closest to God when surrounded by nature, marveling at the beauty of His creation.

When we understand our spiritual pathway, it helps us create habits and practices that nurture our relationship with God in a way that feels natural and fulfilling. So if we can be spiritually fed doing activities outside of church on Sunday, what is the meaning of church? And what is church?

Let's first look at my friend Maggie's story: She loved spending Sunday mornings hiking. She shared with me that with every step on the trail, enveloped by nature, she felt closer to God. It was her sanctuary, a place where she prayed, reflected, and felt at peace. For years, she believed this was enough.

Then her life took an unexpected turn. After a difficult breakup and the loss of her job, Maggie felt adrift. Her hikes, which were once a source of peace, started to feel hollow. The solitude she had once cherished magnified her loneliness. I invited her to church, and she was hesitant, but agreed to come.

What Maggie found surprised her. It wasn't the music or the message that moved her most; it was the people. When she opened up enough to share her struggles, they didn't just offer kind words; they listened to understand, surrounded her with prayer, and helped her search for new job opportunities. Over time, she realized that her faith, though deeply personal, was never meant to be lived in isolation. Maggie still hikes on Sundays occasionally, but now it's different. She knows that her faith grows deepest when it's rooted in community.

Personal spiritual practices like hiking, prayer, or reading are meaningful, but they cannot replace the communal nature of the church. The church is where we embody the relational design of our participatory universe, living out faith not in isolation but in connection. I think many of us have distanced ourselves because of wounds inflicted by someone who professed to be a Christian. They may have even been a leader in the church you grew up in.

Church Hurt: Finding Trust and Faith Again

Trust and faith go hand in hand; they are the foundation of any relationship. Yet, life—like a stock market chart—is rarely a straight line. As a wealth manager, I often use these charts to show the overall upward trend over decades, despite the highs and lows, the peaks and valleys along the way. Our spiritual lives follow a similar path. Faith isn't smooth or linear; it's marked by questions, doubts, and challenges. But this is how we're designed: We are to think, to inquire, and to seek. God never promised an easy journey, but He does assure us it has purpose. The book of James reminds you to *"consider it pure joy . . . whenever you face trials of many kinds, because the testing of your faith produces perseverance"* (James 1:2–4 NIV).

Still, few things test our faith like church hurt. It can anchor us to a single painful moment or season, shaping how we view Jesus, His church, and even our faith itself. To better understand this, let me draw a parallel from my world of wealth management. Behavioral finance is a field that explores how our emotions and mental habits influence the way we handle money. It studies why we sometimes make decisions about spending, saving, or investing that aren't logical. These decisions are often driven by emotional biases. One of the key concepts in this field is called availability bias, which is our tendency to focus on the most vivid or emotionally charged experiences when making judgments, even if they don't represent the bigger picture.

For example, an investor sees her portfolio drop in value and panics. Even though she's had years of growth, she can't stop thinking about the fear she felt in 2008 when the market crashed. That memory becomes her anchor, distorting her perspective. She forgets the sound strategies that brought her success, like staying the course, owning solid investments, and giving time for growth.

In much the same way, many of us anchor our view of God to a painful church experience. Maybe it was a teaching that felt wrong, questions that went unanswered, or unethical behavior by church leaders. Perhaps someone in the church, a self-professed Christian no less, hurt us deeply, leaving us disillusioned. Those moments become all we can see, distorting our perception of God and His people. We focus on the pain, and the case for Jesus is closed.

But what if, like an investor, we could step back, zoom out, and look at the bigger picture? What if we allowed God to rewrite the story of our faith, even after seasons of hurt? I believe healing begins with understanding the depth of our unity in Christ.

Why the Church Is Essential

The word translated as "church" in the Bible is *ekklesia*. In Greek, it comes from *kaleo* (to call) with the prefix *ek* (out), which literally means "called out ones." Over time, this word came to mean "church" in English. It came to be associated with a physical building, marked by a cross, where people meet on Sunday mornings.[58] But the original meaning wasn't about a building; it was about a group of people. Not a *what*, a *who*.

Not a *where*, a *who*. We are the church—God's people, called by Him, loved by Him, and chosen to follow Him. The *ekklesia* is about gathering together, a community united by faith and purpose. It's not about walls or pews; it's about the people who come together to live out God's love.

There are three key reasons why gathering as a community is so important:

- Being part of the body of Christ allows us to experience the beauty and power of how God moves through His people when they come together.
- The healing and freedom that come through group confession, which we'll explore more in the next chapter.
- Helping and encouraging one another, reminding each other of God's faithfulness through shared stories of His goodness, both from the past and in our lives today.

The Body of Christ

In chapter 6, we talked about the Latin word *potere*, which means "to be able," and how reflecting on God's limitless power can remind us of who He is and what He's done. This helps us feel capable through Him. Interestingly, another word that comes from the same root is *posse*, which we use today to mean a group of friends or a team. Originally though, it carried the idea of collective power; a united group working as one.[59] It meant people coming together with shared ability or purpose.

The Apostle Paul offers a powerful metaphor for this unity: the body of Christ. In 1 Corinthians 12:12, 26–27, he describes the church as a body, with many parts working together as one:

> *The human body has many parts, but the many parts make up one whole body. So it is with the body of Christ. . . . If one part suffers, all the parts suffer with it, and if one part is honored, all the parts are glad. All of you together are Christ's body, and each of you is a part of it.*

Just as our physical bodies rely on every organ and limb to function properly, the body of Christ depends on each of us to fulfill our unique roles.

In the body of Christ, we are united into one family, regardless of background or social standing. Earthly divisions like ethnicity, gender, or status do not define one's relationship with Christ:

> *For there is one body and one Spirit, just as you have been called to one glorious hope for the future. There is one Lord, one faith, one **baptism, one God and Father of all, who is over all, in all, and living through all.***
>
> —Ephesians 4:4–6 (emphasis added)

The church is essential because it is more than a collection of individuals seeking God on their own terms. The body of Christ is a living, breathing organism where faith is shared, nurtured, and lived out in unity. It's where faith becomes real as we share

Christ's love, care for one another, and worship together. It's not just about believing—it's about belonging to something far greater than ourselves.

The Healing Power of Group Confession

Confession brings a kind of healing and freedom that can't be found anywhere else. We'll get more into this in the next chapter. But here's something to consider now: People in the church are not perfect. And, we're hypocrites. We'll also disappoint you. Both inside and outside the church, we can't escape who and what we are: humans in need of grace.

But I choose to walk alongside those who embrace this truth, knowing they are forgiven when they confess and strive to do better. Avoiding the community of the church, especially the accountability that comes with personal recollection and group confession, often means running from something. Without accountability, there is no growth.

If you're part of a church where humility and honesty aren't welcome, it's time to leave. Appearances do no one any good in the life of Christ. A healthy church is marked by humility, honesty, and an awareness of our need for forgiveness.

Helping and Encouraging One Another

In Christ, each of us is uniquely gifted to help and encourage one another (1 Corinthians 12:7). Life can feel heavy, and the more relationships we have, the more we may feel the weight of life's burdens. Yet, this is where the church shines: We have the power of God to pour courage into one another. We can remind each other of who God is, what He's done, and the hope we have in Him.

While we may not always see the immediate results of our efforts, we can trust that God is working through us in ways beyond our understanding. Sometimes, He blesses us with glimpses of the impact we've had, whether through an encouraging word, a kind action, or simply being present in someone's life. That's the beauty of the church. It's not about standing on the sidelines. We are active participants in God's story, working together to strengthen and uplift one another as we live out His purpose on Earth.

Church: Where We Live Out the Natural Order of Love

There's a natural order to love, and it begins with knowing that God loves you no matter what. When you truly understand this, it changes how you see yourself. You begin to see yourself the way God does: valued and cherished. From that place of fullness, you're able to love others, knowing God loves them just as much as He loves you.

You can't truly love others if you don't love yourself. And real self-love comes from understanding that you are loved by God. *"This is real love—not that we loved God, but that he loved us and sent his Son as a sacrifice to take away our sins"* (1 John 4:10). *"We love each other because he loved us first"* (1 John 4:19). God calls us to the kind of love that transforms how we see ourselves and others.

Think of it this way: Everything in the universe is connected. Quantum theory explains this on a physical level, but it's also true spiritually. Love is the invisible thread that holds us together. It's woven into every interaction, every relationship, and every moment of our lives.

When we get the order right: loving God first, letting His love shape how we see ourselves, and then sharing that love with others, we align with God's plan for the world. It starts with love, and it ends with love. That's what holds it all together.

In our participatory universe, nothing exists in isolation. Just as quantum mechanics reveals that identity arises through interaction, so our spiritual lives find meaning through relationships with God and with others. The Trinity shows us that our lives, our faith, and our purpose thrive when we embrace connection. Alone, we see glimpses of God's handiwork. But together, we participate in the fullness of His divine plan. The wonder of it all is that in Christ, we are united to God and one another, living out the relational design for which we were created.

Before we begin our next chapter on finding margin in our lives, let's get to this week's activities.

Activities Week 10

Heart (physical exercise): Upon waking, do the child's pose with gratitude. Then, do a two-part hip and lower back release.

First, perform rolls by sitting cross-legged on the floor or with a bolster/cushion under your seat (if you have knee sensitivities). Place your palms on your knees, sit up tall, and relax your shoulders. Perform rolls five to ten times in one direction then change directions by making a circle: leaning forward, then to the left, then back and to the right.

Second, after rolling, place your hands on the floor in front of you and walk your fingers forward as you fold over and relax your neck and head down. Stay anywhere from five to ten breaths. Then, walk your fingers over to the right (where your heart is reaching out over your right knee), breathe. Then to the other side.

Mind (cleanse): Sit in a comfortable position and practice diminishing prayer meditation, letting the words *"Be still and know that I am God" from* Psalm 46:10 sink into you.

> "Be still and know that I am God.
> Be still and know that I am.
> Be still and know.
> Be still.
> Be."

Soul (renew and restore): Reflect and write down which spiritual pathways (intellectual, relational, serving, worship, activist, contemplative, creation) speak to you most. Think how you'll incorporate those into your week.

Loving Others (scripture and prayer): Read Paul's prayer for spiritual growth in Ephesians 3:14–21:

> *When I think of all this, I fall to my knees and pray to the Father, the Creator of everything in heaven and on earth. I pray that from his glorious, unlimited resources he will empower you with inner strength through his Spirit. Then Christ will make his home in your hearts as you trust in him. Your roots will grow down into God's love and keep you strong. And*

may you have the power to understand, as all God's people should, how wide, how long, how high, and how deep his love is. May you experience the love of Christ, though it is too great to understand fully. Then you will be made complete with all the fullness of life and power that comes from God. Now all glory to God, who is able, through his mighty power at work within us, to accomplish infinitely more than we might ask or think. Glory to him in the church and in Christ Jesus through all generations forever and ever! Amen.

CHAPTER 11:
SUBTRACTION AND THE ART OF LETTING GO

Truth is ever to be found in the simplicity, and not in the multiplicity and confusion of things.

—Sir Isaac Newton

Marie Kondo reached fame by inspiring millions to purge their closets and organize their lives. Her famous mantra, "Does it spark joy?"[60] became a touchstone for people navigating through the clutter in their homes and minds. By asking this question, she guided them from feeling heavy, overwhelmed, and stuck to feeling light, free, and ready to move forward. Kondo's approach wasn't just about tidying up; it was about helping people cut ties with what no longer served them, bringing intention and clarity to their lives. Cleaning out a closet became a metaphor for stepping into a fresh, joyful, and purposeful version of themselves.

I write this chapter at the beginning of January, fresh off the whirlwind of crossing everything off my Christmas to-do list, attending December parties, and reflecting on a full year of hard work.

I hit a breaking point before I arrived here though: the moment when you know it's time to purge, and the burden of not doing it has been weighing you down. For me, it was the chaos in my home office. Tucked away in the closet of my serene yoga and reading room, the clutter was a stark contrast to the calm I craved. Those overflowing files weren't just physical; they reflected how overwhelmed I felt emotionally and mentally.

So on New Year's Eve, I dove in. Five hours and five bags of paper later, I could see my desk again. With the clutter gone, I felt lighter, freer, and ready to tackle my new year, and the rest of my life, with clarity and intention.

Who doesn't love the New Year? It brings a sense of renewal and possibility. For a few weeks, the culture around us encourages us to simplify, prioritize, and live with intention. But by the end of January, the energy fades, life gets busy, and good intentions get buried until the next New Year's wave comes around.

This cycle reveals a deeper truth: We often crave more. We accumulate possessions, commitments, and worries, until the weight feels unbearable. But what if we embraced a lifestyle of subtraction instead? By humbly recognizing what no longer serves us on a regular basis and letting it go, we create space to focus on what truly matters.

When I make room in my life, whether in my schedule, my mind, or my heart, I'm no longer rushing or overwhelmed. I have time to be present, to connect, and to savor life's simple joys.

Subtraction isn't just about less; it's about intentionally making room for the things and people that truly matter to each of us.

The Cost of A Hurried Life

Malcolm Gladwell, in his book *The Tipping Point*,[61] highlights a fascinating study on how being rushed impacts our behavior and how we treat others. Inspired by the biblical story of the Good Samaritan, where only one man stopped to help a beaten and robbed traveler while others passed by, two Princeton psychologists set out to replicate the scenario.

As Gladwell tells it, seminary students were asked to prepare a talk on either the parable of the Good Samaritan or the role of clergy in religious life. Then, they were instructed to walk to a nearby building to deliver their presentation. Along the way, each student encountered a man slumped in an alley, coughing and groaning. Who would stop to help him?

The results surprised everyone. It wasn't their theology, their motivation for studying ministry, or even being reminded of the parable that influenced their behavior. The only factor that mattered was whether they were in a rush. Students who were told, "You're late," almost always hurried past, with only 10 percent stopping to help. In contrast, when students knew they had a few minutes to spare, 63 percent stopped to care for the man.

The conclusion of the study is sobering: The convictions in our hearts and the thoughts in our minds often take a back seat to the immediate context of our lives. Just hearing the words *"You're late"* turned well-meaning students into people indifferent to someone in need. It's a powerful reminder that when we live hurried lives, we may not be living up to the people we think we are or the people we truly want to be.

External pressures can undermine humility and integrity. In this story, it wasn't the moral convictions that determined whether seminary students stopped to help. But being in a rush revealed how easy it is to stray from our ideals when overwhelmed by the demands of our environment. Even those reflecting on the Good Samaritan parable struggled to live out its teachings when pressed for time. It demonstrates how situational factors can disrupt our harmony with who we aim to be.

In our fast-paced world, this story challenges us to think about how we manage our time and attention. Are we rushing past opportunities that could make a difference? Are we truly living in alignment with the ideals we hold dear? The lesson here goes beyond helping a stranger. It's about creating space in our lives to notice and respond to the humanity around us. Living with integrity requires more than good intentions; it demands we slow down, acknowledging that we are all susceptible to lapses in judgment. By prioritizing presence over being rushed, we can better ensure that our actions reflect the ideals and values we hold close to heart.

Freedom Through Humility

As Rick Warren put it, "Humility is not thinking less of yourself, it's thinking of yourself less."[62]

Humility is a quality we often admire but rarely find easy to practice. Opportunities to embrace it come up often in our everyday lives, particularly as we grow and face more situations that challenge our ego. My girlfriend Melanie and I recently agreed that one of the most admirable traits in a person is their ability to receive correction and adjust their attitude. There's something liberating, even inspiring about witnessing someone acknowledge when they are wrong or when their behavior hurts others. But getting to that point requires something profound: the death of the ego.

Why is this so difficult for us? We're naturally resistant, clinging to our own perspectives and justifying our actions, even when they conflict with the truth. The idea of living with integrity and authenticity is appealing, yet when the moment comes to act on it, it can feel impossibly hard. Our egos, or false selves—the parts of us disconnected from God—march ahead with glitter and gold, blinding us to the freedom that comes with humility. Recognizing and dismantling these barriers is the first step toward living with integrity and aligning ourselves with God's truth.

In Matthew 5, Jesus begins the Sermon on the Mount with, *"Blessed are the poor in spirit, for theirs is the kingdom of heaven"* (Matthew 5:3). This teaching reminds us that humility is foundational. Before God, we bring nothing to the table; we are entirely reliant on His grace. Romans 11:34 reinforces this truth: *"Who has known the mind of the Lord, or who has been his counselor?"* By staying connected to God, we can set aside our pride, embrace humility, and allow His goodness to guide us.

Humility starts on the inside. The fruit of it is integrity. And when someone lives with integrity, you can see God's goodness shine through in their choices. Integrity is the man at a work conference who faces a choice: he could cheat on his spouse, knowing no one would find out. But he would know.

In that moment, he chooses faithfulness over secrecy—and that's enough to keep him on the right path. Integrity is the woman tempted by envy, swiping her credit card on makeup, designer clothes, and tattoos while her bank balance sits at just $200. She could keep spending recklessly. Instead, she takes responsibility, reads Dave Ramsey's financial guidance, and transforms her mindset—choosing financial wisdom over impulse. Integrity is the woman who fills her schedule to avoid facing her pain, leaving a trail of broken promises and straining her relationships. She could continue running. But instead, she stops, acknowledges her struggles, re-prioritizes her life, and humbly repairs what was damaged. Integrity is the husband whose marriage is crumbling under the weight of his drinking. He could deny it, make excuses, and keep going down the same path. Instead, he joins AA, admits he's not in control, and chooses sobriety—putting his family first.

These are all critical turning points. Moments when people decide to get honest with themselves and make a change. It comes down to the math: one degree of separation from integrity leads to a complete off-course years down the road. But these folks did an about-face before it was too late. When we choose to face the truth, take responsibility, and make changes, we become stronger for the next challenge. And the best part is our choices don't just lift us up, they also lift up the people around us.

The Subtlety of Conviction

Conviction often serves as the turning point toward humility. It begins with an inner recognition that our thoughts, choices, or actions have strayed from God's way. This personal reflection feels unsettling as it forces us to confront the reality of our shortcomings. But conviction isn't about condemnation. It's God's way of inviting us to realign with His truth and experience the freedom that comes with it.

Here's a moment from my own life that might help explain this. Recently, during a moment of quiet meditation, a thought emerged that left me feeling bothered. I realized that I had awakened in the middle of the night with the same thought and feeling just hours before, but at the time, I brushed it off and went back to sleep. The funny thing is that my unsettled feeling came from something small: a casual conversation with a friend about their kids. My friend had shared how their school year ended on a high note, with great grades and how proud he and his wife were of their hard work. I was genuinely happy for them while we talked, but apparently, something lodged itself in my subconscious. And if I hadn't taken the time to sit quietly and reflect, that little seed would've grown into something much bigger.

You see, my daughter has severe dyslexia and struggles in school. She works so hard but still has to see a word about forty times before it sticks, whereas others, like my friend's children, might only need to see it once or twice. As I sat there, it hit me: I was jealous. A little twinge of comparison and frustration had crept in. God used that quiet moment to reveal my spirit of jealousy and discontentment, so He could prune it. This was a much-needed subtraction; God replaced the weight of jealousy with the lightness that comes through His goodness and peace.

When we choose not to ignore these moments and allow God to work within us, conviction becomes a gift. It brings clarity and leads us to confession, where we can release what weighs us down and step fully into His grace.

Confession, then, is the outward expression of our humility. It's the act of acknowledging to ourselves and to others where we've gone astray. This process frees us from the burdens of pride and pretense, giving us the strength to walk in integrity. Whether it's the man who resists infidelity, the woman who overhauls her spending habits, or the parent who admits their addiction and begins the hard work of recovery, the path begins with an honest confession of what's been hidden or ignored. In confession, we find freedom, as it allows us to reconcile our actions with our values.

Life is a continual training ground for humility, where conviction leads us to moments of self-awareness and courage. By reflecting on our actions and confessing our missteps, we open ourselves to the freedom of living with integrity.

The Enemies Working against Us

We can't talk anymore about confession without first addressing sin. The way I understand sin best is that it's a state of separation from God, where reconciliation is impossible through our actions alone. With that in mind, it is crucial to recognize who and what have a vested interest in keeping that separation intact.

John Mark Comer, in his book *Live No Lies*,[63] identifies three key enemies that sabotage our peace and keep us disconnected from God's presence:

- **The Flesh** – the selfish desires in our hearts, thoughts, words, or actions.
- **The World** – the patterns and systems we live in that normalize and perpetuate sin.

- **The Devil** – a real, fallen angel with an army intent on battling God by destroying what He values most, which by now you know is us.

I know this might sound extreme. But let me remind you, my friends, things aren't always what they seem. And I do not think we should be limiting the things of this world to only what's observable. In other words, the flesh, the world, and the devil are the three root sources of sin. And here's the hard truth: We are naturally drawn to them, like moths to a flame.

And that's the problem. There's an unseen battle raging in us and around us. Yet most of us are not only blind to the attack, but we also don't even realize we're in the fight. Recognizing these enemies starts with understanding the internal process that leads us to sin. Ruth Bell Graham describes it in three steps:

1. **Contemplation** – entertaining the thought of sin.
2. **Rationalization** – justifying why it's okay.
3. **Consent** – giving in and acting on it.

She adds a sharp PS: "Sin always affects others."[64]

King David's Confession

Now let me summarize the horrendous story of King David and Uriah found in 2 Samuel chapters 11 and 12. It clearly shows how sin can spiral out of control.

While his army is off at war, David sees Bathsheba, the wife of Uriah, one of his mighty men, bathing, and David can't resist his desire. He summons her to the palace, sleeps with her, and guess what—she ends up pregnant. To cover it up, David calls Uriah back from the battlefield in hopes that he will go home to spend the night with his wife. Then everyone would think the baby was his.

But Uriah is a man of integrity. He refuses to enjoy the comforts of his wife and home while his fellow soldiers are still out fighting. So when that plan fails, David moves to plan B: He sends Uriah to the front lines with orders to place him in the most dangerous spot, practically guaranteeing he'd be killed. After Uriah dies, David takes Bathsheba as his wife.

David moves on, and God sends the prophet Nathan to confront him. Nathan tells David this short story: There was a rich man with plenty of sheep and a poor man with only one lamb he loved like family. When the rich man needed to feed a guest, he took the poor man's lamb instead of one from his own flock. David hears the story, is furious, and says, "The rich man deserves to die for what he has done." Then Nathan drops the truth bomb: "You are that man." David immediately realizes he has messed up big time and confesses, saying, "I've sinned against the Lord."

Nathan assures King David that God has forgiven him, but there will still be consequences for his actions, including hardship within his family. There's always a cost for bad choices. Even still, this is the moment David is willing to own up to his mistakes and seek forgiveness even though he is a powerful king.

Releasing guilt through repentance paves the way for renewal and a restored relationship with God. David's deep desire for forgiveness and a fresh start is beautifully expressed in Psalm 51. In verses 10–11, he pleads: *"Create in me a clean heart, O God. Renew a loyal spirit within me. Do not banish me from your presence, and don't take your Holy Spirit from me. Restore to me the joy of your salvation."*

David's words remind us that true repentance not only brings forgiveness but also rekindles the joy and connection we find in God's grace.

Letting Go of Burdens and Distractions

I have a few girlfriends that I can tell everything to—all the things you're not supposed to say out loud. They listen without judgment, and something amazing happens when I confess. Speaking my hidden thoughts takes away their power. My friends remind me I'm not alone and point me to God's forgiveness. I feel lighter and stronger.

Confession sounds like an old churchy word, because it is. Its history from the Latin goes back to the 1400s meaning "to admit;" "to acknowledge;" or "to speak, tell, or say."[65] But it's a powerful tool for freedom. As mentioned in an earlier chapter, you can start by asking yourself: What's bothering me? The things that weigh on us can pull us away from God's presence. And like a closet getting too full by the end of the year, bothers pile up. They're cumulative. But recognizing and releasing them brings healing.

In the past, people confessed to priests. Today, many turn to therapists. Both offer incredible value. Whether in a spiritual or therapeutic setting, confession helps uncover burdens, offering clarity, strength, and a renewed sense of freedom.

Examen Prayer: A Powerful Practice for Daily Renewal

The early church practiced something called "Examen Prayer," a tradition that might sound archaic but carries immense power. With pressures growing heavier every day, it's high time to bring this daily habit back.

Here's how it works: Set aside fifteen minutes at the end of your day. Go for a walk without earbuds, podcasts, or distractions. Just solitude and quiet. You could also sit and have a journal at the ready. Treat this time as an appointment with God, a time to talk with the Great Counselor and Physician:

1. **Reflect on the Highs:** Start by scanning through your day and ask yourself: When did I feel God's presence the most? Reflect on moments of goodness, joy, peace, or gratitude. Where were you, what happened, and who were you with? How did God reveal Himself in that moment? This could be something as subtle as seeing your children first thing in the morning, healthy, and getting them off to school safely, or it could be a stranger's smile as you crossed paths. Let yourself notice both the subtle and not-so-subtle gifts or miracles God gave you that day.

2. **Reflect on the Lows:** Next, consider what bothered you. What weighed on your heart? Why is it bothering you, and who was involved in that experience? Reflect on how you might handle it differently and what kind of outcome you hope for. Then, visualize placing the entire situation in God's hands, trusting Him to work through it for His glory in your life and others' lives.

The range of outcomes of Examen Prayer are limitless, and it allows God to bring light into the dark corners of your heart and mind. You might gain guidance, clarity, or a deeper understanding of yourself. Perhaps He will show you a way to reconcile a work conflict, soften your heart toward someone, or confront an unhealthy habit. Sometimes, it's subtle; for example, you might realize that you've let social media cloud your priorities. Or maybe it's more serious, like recognizing a moral failure. Whatever comes to the surface, trust that God is gently shaping you for the better.

By creating a daily habit in this practice, you're making space for gratitude, confession, and renewal. It reminds us that God is with us in every moment and invites us to return to Him when we've strayed. Confession becomes an act of subtraction. We're acknowledging where we've fallen short and releasing the guilt or shame that burdens us. In its place, God pours out grace, offering renewal and a deeper connection with Him.

The Art of Forgiveness

Both apologizing and forgiving are hard. Anger and pain have a way of sticking around, and if we're not careful, they can take over. Even when someone says, "I'm sorry" or you say, "I forgive you," it can feel like something's still left undone. "Forgive and forget" sounds nice, but let's be real, forgetting isn't always possible, and forgiveness takes real work.

One story that sticks with me is from the movie *The Machinist*.[66] Christian Bale's character, Trevor, is haunted by guilt so much that he can't sleep; he starts hallucinating and wastes away to nothing. By the end, you learn that his entire life was wrecked because of a tragedy he never faced. This is a fictional example, but it shows how guilt or unresolved pain can consume us when we don't deal with it.

True forgiveness is freeing. It doesn't mean excusing someone's behavior or pretending the hurt didn't happen. It's about getting to a place where the memory doesn't hold power over you anymore. It's about finding peace in your own heart and letting go of the bitterness or anger weighing you down. Forgiveness doesn't mean that the pain didn't matter; it just means it doesn't control you anymore.

But forgiveness isn't always about someone else. Sometimes, it's about forgiving ourselves. During my shingles experience I listed, "forgive myself daily" as an item that needed addressing, though I wasn't even sure what it meant. Forgive myself for what? As I sat with it, I realized it wasn't about one specific thing. It was about letting go of years of unrealistic expectations, pressure to achieve, perfectionism, and high demands on myself and others. It was about releasing the weight I thought I carried for other people and accepting that God's grace is enough. Jesus's words, *"My grace is sufficient for you"* (2 Corinthians 12:9 NIV) became my daily mantra. Forgiveness felt like finally being able to breathe.

Forgiveness takes many forms. For some, it means letting go of deep wounds caused by others. For others, it's about learning to be gentle with themselves. But one thing is clear: Whether forgiving someone else or yourself, it matters. The Bible reminds us that we are all in need of forgiveness. Every wrong, whether intentional or not, is inexcusable before God. But through Jesus, we're set free. This forgiveness is the foundation of our faith. When we understand the depth of His love and grace, it overflows, making it possible to extend that same forgiveness to others.

Forgiveness also creates space for healing. Resentment and bitterness take up so much emotional and mental energy. They leave no room for joy, for peace, or for the love God wants us to feel. Forgiveness clears that space. It allows us to let God in, to heal, to redirect our hearts to what matters most: our relationships with Him and with others.

Forgiveness isn't easy. It's not a one-time act. It's a process, a practice. It's the daily choice to let go of what weighs us down. And when we do, we find freedom, not just for others, but for ourselves. We find the blessing of peace, grace, and the overwhelming love of God. That's the art of forgiveness. It's not just for them; it's for you too.

Space for the Soul to Breathe

Confession, forgiveness, and simplicity all work together to create space for the soul to breathe. Whether with too many possessions, packed schedules, or unresolved emotions, when our lives are cluttered, it's hard to find the time or energy for reflection and healing. Confession gives us the quiet moments we need to be honest with ourselves and with God. Forgiveness helps us let go of resentment and bitterness. And simplicity clears away the distractions that keep us from focusing on what matters most. By letting go of the excess, whether it's physical or emotional, we create margin for joy, relationships, and purpose. This process of both practical and spiritual subtraction makes room for grace and renewal.

Loving our neighbors as ourselves starts with humility. Sometimes it comes through reflection, and other times, life forces it on us. Either way, humility gives us the chance to be honest about who we are. It opens the door for forgiveness, both for ourselves and for others, and it helps us choose integrity over pride. When we take that step, we turn away from the destructive habits that harm us and the people around us and move toward healing.

There's an invisible battle happening, and we're in the middle of it. Do you feel it? The world, the flesh, and the devil are constantly trying to pull us off course. But the first step in fighting back is paying attention to what's bothering you. Take a moment to ask yourself where the weight is coming from. Is it guilt? A grudge? Resentment? Bitterness? Imagine handing the whole thing over to God, letting Him take control of the situation. He can help you see where you might need to confess, forgive, or change your perspective. Through His forgiveness, He sets you free and brings you closer to Him.

Activities Week 11

Heart (physical exercise): Upon waking, do the child's pose with gratitude. Then do round 2 of the spine lubrication stretches.

- *Cat/cow:* On your hands and knees (knees below your hips, hands below your shoulders), inhale and draw your pelvis to the sky, taking along with it the spine as it arches up gently through to the neck. Then, exhale as your pelvis tucks in as if drawing toward your

naval, the spine follows and rounds like a rainbow, and you tuck your chin into your chest. Repeat eight to ten times.
- *Lateral stretch (side to side):* Sit cross-legged (on a bolster or pillow if knees are tender) or on a chair. Inhale and raise your arms near your ears. Exhale. Reach your left arm up and over, stretching your left side body long and gently place your right hand onto the floor (not crunching your right side, but lifting your bottom ribs away from your right hip). Breathe a few long deep breaths before changing sides.
- *Rotation (twist):* Lie on your back and draw your knees into your chest. Then, gently drop your legs over to the left side, opening your arms out wide to the side (in one with your shoulders) and look over to your right arm. Breathe a few long deep breaths before changing sides.

Mind (cleanse): Practice the Examen Prayer while out walking today or before bed.

Soul (rest and renew): Take some time to reflect on the people you surround yourself with the most. Write down twelve names, starting with the three you lean on the most, those you trust deeply and share life's burdens and joys with. Then expand to others who make up your closest circle. Ask yourself: Do they uplift and encourage me, helping shape me into the person I'm becoming? Is there a healthy balance of giving and receiving in the relationship? Do their values align with mine, or do they create tension and conflict? Consider whether anyone on the list is an emotional drain, consistently negative, or lacking reciprocity. This exercise isn't about judgment but about fostering a community that supports your growth, aligns with your purpose, and encourages you to live in alignment with God's design for your life.

Loving Others (scripture and prayer): Read Psalm 103 quietly, to yourself. Let it be your prayer.

CHAPTER 12:
GENEROSITY AND BLESSINGS

In his hand is the life of every creature and the breath of all mankind.

—Job 12:10

The journey through this book began with understanding how living fully requires care and attention to every part of our being. We honor God in the way we live, think, and care for ourselves. The practices of rest, nourishment, and movement that sustain our physical health also mirror those for our emotional and spiritual well-being. Just as the body needs sleep to recharge, the spirit needs rest in God through prayer and reflection. Healthy food nourishes the body, while Scripture and time with God feed the soul. Physical exercise strengthens the body, while acts of love, forgiveness, and generosity strengthen the heart and mind.

By tending to all parts of ourselves—body, mind, and soul—we create balance and harmony, enabling us to live with greater purpose. Honoring God involves every aspect of our lives. When we care for our bodies, we gain the physical capacity to serve Him and others. When we nurture our emotional health through forgiveness and simplicity, we shed burdens that hold us back. And when we commit to spiritual practices like prayer and confession, we deepen our connection with God and experience His transformative power.

This journey is not about achieving perfection. There will be times when we slip into old habits, feel weighed down by life's challenges, and even wonder where God is. But grace is at the heart of it all. God's forgiveness, love, and guidance are always there, no matter how often we stumble, fall, or feel distant from Him. Surrendering isn't something we do just once: It's a lifelong practice. When we trust God with our brokenness, we open the door for Him to shape and transform us over time.

At the start of this book, I shared that by the end, you'd be able to identify and track the daily and weekly activities that bring you closer to experiencing God's beauty and presence. Now, as you reach the end of this chapter, I encourage you to reflect and create a game plan. What practices and activities resonated most with you? Which ones will you continue to incorporate into your day-to-day life?

Tying It All Together

As we conclude, let's reflect on one final theme: generosity. It brings everything together, extending the work God is doing in us outward into the lives of others.

GENEROSITY AND BLESSINGS

Generosity is one of the most meaningful ways we can reflect God's love. Generosity is not just about giving resources; it's about offering all of ourselves whether our time, talents, treasures, or our whole heart. Generosity connects us to God's heart and opens the door for His blessings to flow through us to others. Whether through acts of service, forgiveness, or financial sacrifice, saying yes to God's call often stretches us, requiring complete reliance on Him. But in these moments of surrender, we discover immense joy and fulfillment.

Two Stories of Radical Generosity
The story of the wealthy young man in Matthew 19:16–22 (paraphrased) illustrates the challenges of surrender. He approaches Jesus, asking what he must do to gain eternal life. Jesus, clearly addressing a deeper issue, first tells him to follow the commandments. When the man insists he has done so, Jesus offers a harder challenge. He tells the man that if he wants to be perfect, he must go and sell his possessions and give the proceeds to the poor; then, Jesus says, he will have treasure in heaven and he can come and follow Him.

The man walks away sad, unable to let go of his wealth. Earthly attachments can prevent us from fully following Christ. Radical generosity isn't just about what we give; it's about trusting God above all else and freeing ourselves from what holds us back. It's in letting go of the temporary that we can embrace the eternal life Jesus offers.

In contrast, the widow's mite in Mark 12:41–44 demonstrates the beauty of sacrificial giving. While others gave large sums from their abundance, a poor widow offered two small coins, which was all she had. Jesus observed her and declared her gift the greatest of all. Why? Because it came from a place of trust and sacrifice. True generosity isn't measured by the size of the gift but by the position of the heart behind it. God values our willingness to give, no matter how small, when it reflects our trust in Him.

Acts of Service

Generosity also comes through service and humility. Jesus modeled this when He washed His disciples' feet and ultimately through His sacrifice on the cross. He showed us that greatness in God's kingdom is found in serving others, not in seeking power or recognition. Acts of service purify the soul by shifting our focus from selfish desires to the needs of others. When we serve with humility, we break down pride, shape our hearts to reflect God's, and grow in empathy and compassion. These are all traits that deepen our relationship with Him and those around us.

Generosity also means being willing to show up, to give of yourself, and to offer what you can, even when you feel unsure or unprepared. I saw this truth come alive in my own life when I was called to Richard's bedside in his final days. Richard was our family's tax preparer for many years. He'd been battling colon cancer, and his wife Patricia shared that he had been placed on hospice care. After a few back-and-forth calls, I felt compelled to visit and pray with him, despite feeling completely unprepared for what I was stepping into.

As I drove to their home, my inadequacy weighed heavily on me. I didn't have the right words or even a clear plan, but

GENEROSITY AND BLESSINGS

I knew this was something I needed to do. So I turned on worship music and called a friend for support. She prayed with me, asking God to guide my steps and fill me with His presence. Armed with that prayer, I entered their home, where Patricia warned me that Richard was only a shadow of the man we had known as a strong, opinionated, and kind person. Despite my uncertainty, I stepped forward, trusting God to meet us in that sacred moment.

Standing at his bedside, I prayed a kingdom prayer—a prayer that called on God's power, glory, and presence to fill that encounter. I prayed not just comfort for him, but for eternity. It was a prayer for surrender—for Richard to embrace Jesus in his final moments. Patricia later shared that he passed within an hour of my visit. She believed the prayer released him, and her voice carried a peace that hadn't been there before.

Just as Richard was released into eternal life, you too can experience release. Whatever burdens you're carrying, whether fear, frustration, injustices, angst, sadness, jealousy, despair, or pain, know that they don't have to define you. God's yoke is easy, His burden is light, and His love for you is unchanging.

Choosing God is a daily act of surrender. It's a radical decision to let go of what holds us back and embrace His call, even when it feels costly. Whether through sacrifice, service, or stepping into someone else's need, generosity reflects the ultimate gift of love that God has given us through Christ. What is God calling you to release, and where is He inviting you to give?

Trusting Him with your whole self—body, mind, and soul—is the ultimate act of faith, and it opens the door to experiencing the fullness of His love and purpose. When you let go and say yes to Him, buckle up for the most unique adventure that only He can give. Starting now. Take the next step. Breathe deeply. Let it all go, and trust Him to carry you forward. This is your moment to truly live.

Returning Home

All paths can lead to Christ. I believe He uses anything and everything to point us to Him. And His love for you is personal. His grace is so huge that try as you might, up to the very end, He will make the cosmos align and put people in your path to make sure you know it.

Every day, it is too easy for us to go our own way. And God respects our freedom. We can freely resist His love. We can also, freely, turn away from His voice. The more we do, the easier it becomes to tune Him out. But by choosing, each day, to return to Him through prayer, reflecting on His words, and leaning on other Jesus followers, we find our way back. When we return, He meets us with strength, peace, protection, and joy. And the beauty of God's love is that no matter how often we drift, He's always waiting to welcome us home.

A Blessing to You

Imagine knocking on a door that opens to a beautifully pristine, glimmering, well-lit room.

From inside, a gentle voice calls, "Come in."

As you step through the doorway, you see Jesus sitting cross-legged on the ground.

He gestures for you to join Him. "Sit down with me," He says warmly. "Let me have a look at you."

GENEROSITY AND BLESSINGS

You sit across from Him, and when you look up, you see pure delight radiating from His eyes.

"Thank you for coming to visit with me today. You bless me by being here. Settle in. I want to give you something," He says.

You let your shoulders relax and rest your hands on your knees, palms turned up. He places His hands around yours, and you take a deep breath in.

As you exhale, His words flow into you: "I bless you, and I protect you. My face shines on you, and my grace is upon you. I give you my favor, and I give you my peace" (Numbers 6:24–26, paraphrased).

These words are more than just sounds. They sink deeply into every cell of your body, filling you with warmth and life. They penetrate your soul, reaching places you didn't even know needed healing. Your spirit holds a newfound readiness to express the unique, divine design of your soul, the very idea of you in the mind of God. In this moment, you are known, loved, and blessed beyond measure.

FINAL WORDS

As you leave that sacred space in your mind, hold onto the truth that Jesus's blessing is not just for a moment; it's for your every moment. His love, His favor, and His peace go with you, wherever you are, whatever you face.

This journey of loving God with all your heart, mind, and soul isn't about perfection, it's about presence. It's about showing up every day with open hands and an open heart, ready to receive His blessings and ready to reflect them into the world around you.

Step into the life God has designed for you with courage and faith. Care for your body as His temple. Renew your mind with His truth. Nourish your soul in His presence. And live as a vital part of His body, connected to others and called to love deeply.

You are uniquely made, uniquely loved, and uniquely called. Go forward, fully alive, fully loved, and fully His.

Blessings on your adventure.

ACKNOWLEDGMENTS

Writing this book has been one of the most rewarding and challenging experiences of my life. I couldn't have done it without the incredible support of so many people.

To my husband and children: Thank you for your endless patience, love, and belief in me.

To my mom and dad: Your constant encouragement and support for everything I set my mind and heart to have always been a source of strength.

To my sister Cameron, Casey, Melanie, and Summer: You have shaped me in ways that words can hardly express.

To Ann Marie: Thank you for walking alongside me in this journey and for reading all the scattered and imperfect beginnings of this project. Your friendship has been a steady anchor in this journey, and I'm forever thankful.

To my Wealthwise Partners team: Your expertise, dedication, and approach to serving our clients have transformed countless lives. Relying on your experience and building what we have together has been an honor. Your excellence has also created space in my life for this project to take shape, and I'm deeply grateful.

To Erin, Leah, and all the ladies of Pit Crew: Your spiritual insights and the way you've spoken into my life have helped form this book.

To Amy Bailey, Brittany Baer, and the team at The Stirring: Your ministry and mentorship have profoundly influenced my journey.

To the professors at Concordia University, Irvine, and my Macau mission team, especially Melissa Chew: You poured into me and imprinted my heart forever. To Barbara Gunter, Rendy Koeppel, and Pastor Prange: Thank you for planting the seed and nurturing deep roots of faith in me at Mt. Calvary Lutheran. Pastor Stace and Karen Rollefson: Your love for God and service to others stands out among the rest. To Pastor Travis at VC Family: Thank you for your relatable and impactful way of bringing Jesus to the Redding, California community.

To Josh Tyra, for sharing your incredible translation skills with me. To Roseanne Cheng: Your guidance on this project from the very beginning has been invaluable, and I can't thank you enough.

To Jennifer Galardi, Aaron Hayes, and Alison Hall: Thank you for your willingness to be early copyreaders and for helping shape this book.

Heartfelt thanks to the team at Lucid Publishing for your guidance and belief in this project from the start.

To Jesse Moffet for the beautiful cover design.

And finally, to you, dear reader: Thank you for opening these pages. My prayer is that this book blesses you and draws you closer to the heart of God.

ENDNOTES

1 Lewis Carroll, *Alice's Adventures in Wonderland*, illustrated by John Tenniel (Macmillan, 1865).
2 Dallas Willard with John Ortberg, *Living in Christ's Presence: Final Words on Heaven and the Kingdom of God*, narrated by Dallas Willard (christianaudio.com, 2014).
3 Richard J. Foster, *Celebration of Discipline: The Path to Spiritual Growth* (Harper & Row, 1978).
4 Henry David Thoreau, *Walden or Life in the Woods* (Ticknor and Fields, 1854).
5 Dallas Willard, *The Great Omission: Reclaiming Jesus's Essential Teachings on Discipleship* (HarperOne, 2006), 89.
6 Barry Sears, *Enter the Zone: A Dietary Road Map* (HarperCollins, 1995).
7 Erin Donnelly Michos, "Sitting Disease: How a Sedentary Lifestyle Affects Heart Health," Johns Hopkins Medicine—Health, accessed January 2025, https://www.hopkinsmedicine.org/health/wellness-and-prevention/sitting-disease-how-a-sedentary-lifestyle-affects-heart-health.
8 Curt Thompson, *Anatomy of the Soul: Surprising Connections Between Neuroscience and Spiritual Practices That Can Transform Your Life and Relationships*, narrated by Sean Pratt (Tantor Audio, 2016).

9   J. R. Yoginidra, "50 Blissful Yoga Statistics for 2024," yogaearth.com, January 27, 2024, https://yogaearth.com/yoga-research/yoga-statistics.
10 Foster, *Celebration of Discipline*.
11 *Collins English Dictionary*, "Yoke," accessed January 22, 2025, www.collinsdictionary.com/dictionary/english/yoke.
12 *Braveheart*, directed by Mel Gibson (Paramount Pictures, 1995).
13 Ben Keil, *Morning Blessings: A Guide to the Traditional Shachrit (morning) Service*, My Jewish Learning, accessed January 2025, https://www.myjewishlearning.com/article/morning-blessings/.
14 Oscar Wilde, *The Picture of Dorian Gray* (Penguin Classics, 2003).
15 *Cambridge Dictionary*, "consciousness," accessed January 2025, https://dictionary.cambridge.org/us/dictionary/english/consciousness.
16 Napoleon Hill, *Think and Grow Rich* (The Ralston Society, 1937).
17 Rickson Gracie and Peter Maguire, *Breathe: A Life in Flow*, narrated by Fred Sanders (HarperAudio, 2021), at 1 hr., 55 min.
18 *Encyclopedia Britannica*, "Sympathetic Nervous System," accessed January 27, 2025, https://www.britannica.com/science/sympathetic-nervous-system.
19 Ashley Turner, "Why You Need to Tend to Your Vagus Nerve," *The Epoch Times*, August 22, 2022, https://www.theepochtimes.com/health/why-you-need-to-tend-to-your-vagus-nerve_4677164.html.

20 *Rudy*, directed by David Anspaugh (TriStar Pictures, 1993).
21 Rudy Ruettiger speaking at a Simpson University Business Luncheon, Redding, California.
22 *Talladega Nights: The Ballad of Ricky Bobby*, directed by Adam McKay (Columbia Pictures, 2006).
23 C. S. Lewis, *The Weight of Glory* (HarperOne, 2001), 26.
24 Lee Iacocca and William Novak, *An Autobiography* (Bantam Books, 1984).
25 Deepak Chopra and David Simon, *The Seven Spiritual Laws of Yoga: A Practical Guide to Healing Body, Mind, and Spirit* (Wiley, 2004), 67.
26 Chopra and Simon, *Seven Spirtitual Laws of Yoga*, 67.
27 Douglas Harper, "Med," *Online Etymology Dictionary*, accessed January 25, 2025, https://www.etymonline.com.
28 Thompson, *Anatomy of the Soul*, 161–162.
29 Thompson, *Anatomy of the Soul*, narrated by Sean Pratt (Tantor Audio, 2016).
30 "Breathwork: What Is It and How Does It Work?" WebMD, accessed January 26, 2025, https://www.webmd.com/balance/what-is-breathwork.
31 Greg Miller, "How Does Breathing Affect Your Brain?" *Smithsonian Magazine*, October 18, 2022, https://www.smithsonianmag.com/science-nature/how-does-breathing-affect-your-brain-180980950/.
32 Wim Hof, *The Wim Hof Method: Activate Your Full Human Potential* (Sounds True, 2020).
33 Jelle Zwaag, Rick Naaktgeboren, Antonius E. van Herwaarden, Peter Pikkers, and Matthijs Kox, "The Effects of Cold Exposure Training and a Breathing Exercise on

the Inflammatory Response in Humans: A Pilot Study," *Psychosomatic Medicine* 84, no. 4 (2022), 457–467.
34. Henri J. M. Nouwen, *The Inner Voice of Love: A Journey Through Anguish to Freedom* (Doubleday, 1996).
35. *Pink Floyd: The Wall*, directed by Alan Parker (MGM/UA Entertainment, 1982).
36. Plato, *The Republic Book VII*, translated by Desmond Lee (Penguin Classics, 2007), 240–248.
37. Andrew Klavan, *The Truth and Beauty: How the Lives and Works of England's Greatest Poets Point the Way to a Deeper Understanding of the Words of Jesus* (Zondervan, 2022), 176.
38. J. P. Moreland, *The Soul: How We Know It's Real and Why It Matters*, narrated by Jim Denison (christianaudio.com, 2020).
39. Arthur Wallis, *God's Chosen Fast: A Spiritual and Practical Guide to Fasting* (CLC Publications, 1968).
40. Susan Gregory, *The Daniel Fast: Feed Your Soul, Strengthen Your Spirit, and Renew Your Body* (Tyndale House Publishers, 2010).
41. Mindy Pelz, *Fast Like a Girl: A Woman's Guide to Using the Healing Power of Fasting to Burn Fat, Boost Energy, and Balance Hormones* (Hay House, 2022).
42. Dallas Willard quoted in John Ortberg, *Soul Keeping: Caring for the Most Important Part of You* (Zondervan, 2014), 39.
43. Tom Rath, *StrengthsFinder 2.0* (Gallup Press, 2007).
44. Ian Morgan Cron and Suzanne Stabile, *The Road Back to You: An Enneagram Journey to Self-Discovery* (InterVarsity Press, 2016).

45 Erwin Raphael McManus, *The Seven Frequencies of Communication: The Hidden Language of Human Connection* (Arena Publishing, 2024).

46 Dan Sullivan and Benjamin Hardy, *10x Is Easier Than 2x: How World-Class Entrepreneurs Achieve More by Doing Less*, narrated by the authors (Hay House Business, 2023).

47 Horatio G. Spafford and Philip P. Bliss. "It Is Well with My Soul," 1873.

48 *Online Etymology Dictionary*, "Ecclesiastes," accessed January 26, 2025, https://www.etymonline.com/word/ecclesiastes.

49 Dallas Willard, "Spiritual Formation in Christ: A Perspective on What It Is and How It Might Be Done," Dallas Willard Ministries, accessed January 26, 2025, https://dwillard.org/resources/articles/spiritual-formation-in-christ-a-perspective-on-what-it-is-and-how-it-might-be-done.

50 Willard, "Spiritual Formation in Christ."

51 Benjamin Hardy and Dan Sullivan, *The Gap and the Gain: The High Achievers' Guide to Happiness, Confidence, and Success* (Hay House Business, 2021).

52 "Socially Isolated People Have Differently Wired Brains and Poorer Cognition," *Neuroscience News*, June 17, 2022, https://neurosciencenews.com/social-isolation-cognition-brain-20857/.

53 Carlo Rovelli, *Reality Is Not What It Seems: The Journey to Quantum Gravity*, translated by Simon Carnell and Erica Segre (Riverhead Books, 2017).

54 *Online Etymology Dictionary*, "Messiah," accessed January 27, 2025, https://www.etymonline.com/word/messiah.

55 Mihaly Csikszentmihalyi, *Flow: The Psychology of Optimal Experience* (Harper & Row, 1990), 103.
56 Henri J. M. Nouwen, *The Return of the Prodigal Son: A Story of Homecoming* (Image Books, 1992).
57 John Ortberg and Ruth Haley Barton, *The Ordinary Day with Jesus: Experiencing the Reality of God in Your Everyday Life* (Zondervan, 2001).
58 "Definition of Ekklesia," GotQuestions.org, accessed January 27, 2025, https://www.gotquestions.org/definition-ekklesia.html.
59 *Online Etymology Dictionary*, "Posse," accessed January 27, 2025, https://www.etymonline.com/word/posse.
60 Marie Kondo, *Spark Joy: An Illustrated Master Class on the Art of Organizing and Tidying Up*, translated by Cathy Hirano (Ten Speed Press, 2016).
61 Malcolm Gladwell, *The Tipping Point: How Little Things Can Make a Big Difference* (Little, Brown, 2000).
62 Rick Warren, *The Purpose Driven Life: What on Earth Am I Here For?* (Zondervan, 2002), 149.
63 John Mark Comer, *Live No Lies: Recognize and Resist the Three Enemies That Sabotage Your Peace* (WaterBrook, 2021), 19.
64 Ruth Bell Graham, *"Weekending" The Women's Devotional Bible* (Zondervan, 1990), 14.
65 *Online Etymology Dictionary*, "Confess," accessed January 27, 2025, https://www.etymonline.com/word/confess.
66 *The Machinist*, directed by Brad Anderson (Paramount Classics, 2004).

Keep Up with the Author

Don't miss a moment—sign up now at www.courtneymcelvain.com to get exclusive updates on author Courtney McElvain's powerful new book, *Invest into Meaning,* and be the first to know when it launches.

www.ingramcontent.com/pod-product-compliance
Lightning Source LLC
Chambersburg PA
CBHW050524170426
43201CB00013B/2073